MISSING BELIEVED KILLED

Woe to the Unwary

Torpedo Airmen

The Strike Wings

Target: Hitler's Oil (with Ronald C. Cooke)

Arctic Airmen (with Ernest Schofield)

Failed to Return

An Illustrated History of the RAF

RAF Records in the PRO (with Simon Fowler,
    Peter Elliott and Christina Goulter)

The Armed Rovers

Eyes of the RAF

The RAF in Camera 1903–1939

The RAF in Camera 1939–1945

The RAF in Camera 1945–1995

RAF Coastal Command in Action 1939–1995

RAF: An Illustrated History from 1918

Britain's Rebel Air Force (with Dudley Cowderoy
    and Andrew Thomas)

The Flight of Rudolf Hess (with Georges van Acker)

RAF in Action 1939–1945

The Battle of Britain

The Battle of the Atlantic

MISSING BELIEVED KILLED

ROY CONYERS NESBIT

SUTTON PUBLISHING

First published in the United Kingdom in 2002 by
Sutton Publishing Limited · Phoenix Mill
Thrupp · Stroud · Gloucestershire · GL5 2BU

British Library Cataloguing in Publication Data
A catalogue record for this book is available from the British Library.

ISBN 0-7509-3003-9

Typeset in 11.5/15pt Garamond.
Typesetting and origination by
Sutton Publishing Limited.
Printed and bound in England by
J.H. Haynes & Co. Ltd, Sparkford.

Contents

Acknowledgements

I am extremely grateful to the large number of friends and colleagues who have helped with the content of the chapters in this book. They are:

Joe Autey; Soloman Belinky USAAF; David Benfield; Fred Biggs RAFVR; Sqn Ldr John A. Botham RAF (Ret'd); Flt Lt Norman D. Boynton RAFVR; Flt Lt Ralph Barker RAF (Retd); John Batchelor; Hugh J. Budgen; Ms Anne Carroll WAAF; WO Bill Carroll RAFVR; Timothy Carroll; The late Air Marshal Sir Edward Chilton KBE, CB; Sqn Ldr Ian Coleman RAF; Sqn Ldr Dudley Cowderoy RAFVR; Ms E. Lettice Curtis ATA; Gordon C. Dalton RAAF; Barry Davidson (Civil Aviation Authority); Chris Davies; Peter Elliott (RAF Museum); John Evans (Peterchurch Publications); Flt Lt Graham Fairhurst RAF (Ret'd); Maurice Fellows; The late Gp Capt Geoffrey Francis DSO, DFC; Frederick M. Galea (National War Museum of Malta); The Late Wg Cdr John C. Graham DFC*; Flt Lt Victor H. Gregory DFC, RAFVR; Brian Hansley; Flt Lt Eric N. Harrison RAFVR (No. 228 Sqn Assn); Gp Capt Charles W. Hayes OBE, RAF (Ret'd); Roger Hayward; Henry Hollway in South Africa; The late Mrs Molly Jones (sister of Amy Johnson); The late Flt Lt Ronald Martin; John A. Miller; The Rev. Fred E. Moore DFC, RAFVR; MEng Phil Nobbs RAF; Michael Oakey (*Aeroplane*); Bob O'Hanlon RAFVR; Capt Hugh O'Neill (Port of London Authority); The late Philip N. Owen RAFVR; Ken Perfect; Capt John Pinder (Port of London Authority); The late Flt Lt A.M. 'Tony' Puckle MBE; Andrew Renwick (RAF Museum); Clive Richards (Air Historical Branch of the MoD); The late Gp Capt F.C. 'Dickie' Richardson CBE, FRIN; Richard Riding (formerly of *Aeroplane Monthly*); Peter Rivers; Bruce Robertson; Alan G. Ross; Mrs Sandra Sanders; Flt Lt Ernest Schofield DFC, RAFVR; Mrs Beryl Seal-Morgan WAAF; The late Fg Off Fred H. Shaw; The late Ms Constance Babington Smith MBE; Tom G. Smith (Rolls-Royce Heritage Trust); Ken Snelling DFC, RAFVR; Halvor Sperbund in Norway; E. Richard Staszak; R. Steiner (de Havilland Heritage Centre); Mrs Adèle Stephenson (airline pilot);

Mrs Bente Mary Sväsand in Norway; Deryck Thurman RAFVR; Dana Timmer (Howland Landing Ltd); Richard T. Tosaw; John Underwood; Adrian Vicary (Maritime Photo Library); Wg Cdr Eric Viles MBE, ATA; Ms Diana Barnato Walker MBE, ATA; Fg Off Bryan Wells RAFVR (RAF Amateur Radio Assn); Cpl Tim Wilson; James A. Woodward RAFVR; Martin Woodward.

Lastly, I should like to thank the two aviation artists who have contributed paintings to this book. They are Martin Postlethwaite GAvA and Charles J. Thompson GAvA, ASAA, GMA, EAA.

CHAPTER ONE

Amelia Earhart

One of the world's most famous aviators, Amelia Earhart, disappeared on 2 July 1937 on a flight from Lae in New Guinea to Howland Island in the Pacific Ocean. Together with her navigator, Fred Noonan, she was nearing the end of her epic attempt to fly round the world on an equatorial route. Their fate has been the subject of enormous speculation since that date, giving rise to a mass of articles, books, and even films.

When the editor of the aviation magazine *Aeroplane Monthly*, Richard Riding, asked me to research this matter, I was doubtful about my ability to find anything new. Then I realised that previous researchers seemed to have concentrated on American records, although much of the flight came under the authority of British civil aviation and the aircraft finally took off from territory which was, at the time, mandated to Australia. Within minutes of beginning my hunt at the Public Record Office in Kew, I discovered material which seemed to have been overlooked by other researchers but which could help resolve what is often regarded as the greatest air mystery of all time. Moreover, some other authors did not seem to have much knowledge of the methods of navigating over vast stretches of ocean, such as astro-navigation, which were of prime importance in 1937 and continued throughout the Second World War. It took several months to complete the necessary research but, in my view, the outcome leaves little room for doubt as to what happened to the aircraft and its occupants. But first it is necessary to relate the events leading up to their disappearance.

Born on 24 July 1898 in Atchinson, Kansas, Amelia Earhart was destined to become the most celebrated woman aviator in America. Her father was Edwin Stanton Earhart, who married Amy Otis on 16 October 1895. Amelia was the elder of their two daughters, with Muriel Grace born two years later. Edwin Earhart was a promising lawyer who worked for the railroad, but his career was impaired by an over-addiction to alcohol. Nevertheless, the family lived in comfortable circumstances, partly supported by Amy's father, Judge Alfred Otis.

Amelia began her working life in a voluntary capacity during the First World War, when she nursed wounded soldiers in a Canadian military hospital in

Toronto. She developed a pacifist philosophy from this experience and also began to espouse the women's liberation movement, in the days before universal suffrage. After the war, she registered as a medical student at Columbia University in New York, but gave up this career to try to help her parents with their marital problems. By this time, they had moved to Los Angeles. In spite of her efforts, the marriage broke up in 1920.

Meanwhile, Amelia had begun to take a keen interest in flying and mechanics, following a trial flight arranged by her father. She took lessons from the woman flyer Neta Snook, paying on an instalment plan. After ten hours of instruction, she went solo in 1921 and then determined to continue training until she obtained a pilot's licence.

Amelia was tall, slender and attractive, with a confident manner, a ready smile and a keen sense of humour. She wore scuffed leather flying jackets and cropped her hair to suit her role as an aviator in a world which was predominantly male. It was said later that she lacked an instinctive feel for the controls of an aircraft, but she certainly possessed qualities of determination and courage which outweighed any deficiencies in that respect. At the time, however, no possibility of flying as a career was available to her. She went to New England, where she became a social worker and also taught basic English to immigrants.

Her first opportunity to achieve fame came in the early summer of 1928 when she agreed to take a place as a passenger and log-keeper on a flight from New York to London. This was in a tri-motored Fokker F.VIIb-3m floatplane named *Friendship*, with Wilmer Stultz as pilot-navigator and Louis Gordon as co-pilot and mechanic. The floatplane took off in the morning of 17 June and arrived at Burry Port in South Wales almost 21 hours later. After a rest and some sleep, they flew on to Southampton and an enthusiastic reception. Although her role in the aircraft had been of limited practical assistance, Amelia thus became the first woman to fly the North Atlantic.

On her return from England, Amelia developed a closer association with one of her admirers. This was George Palmer Putnam, a New York businessman and former publisher, who had met her when she was interviewed for the place in the Fokker. With Putnam's support and enterprise, Amelia left her previous work to improve her flying skills and also to embark on a series of lecture tours arranged by Putnam. These were intended to promote the aircraft industry and to encourage the participation of women in flying. From that time, she was given a great deal of publicity. She became a founder member and president of the 'Ninety-Nines', an organisation consisting initially of that number of women fliers in the USA. Meanwhile, she wrote her first autobiography, *20 hrs 40 min*, mainly concerning her flight across the North Atlantic in the Fokker.

A civic reception for the crew of Fokker F.VIIb-3m *Friendship* on arrival at Southampton on Tuesday 19 June 1928. They had flown from New York to Burry Port in South Wales and then on to Southampton. Centre, left to right: Louis Gordon (co-pilot and mechanic); Amelia Earhart (log-keeper); Wilmer Stultz (pilot-navigator). The floatplane can be seen moored in Southampton Water on the top right, partly obscured by the lady's hat. *(Royal Air Force Museum 4727–9)*

On 22 November 1929, at Burbank in California, Amelia set up a speed record for women in a borrowed Lockheed Vega Executive, a single-engined monoplane. She purchased her own Vega in the following year and in Detroit, Michigan, broke the speed record for a course of 100 km. On 7 February 1931, she and George Putnam were married, shortly after he and his first wife had obtained their divorce. Some commentators regarded the union as more of a business arrangement than a love match, but there does seem to have been genuine affection between the couple.

On 8 April 1931, Amelia broke the altitude record for autogyros. At Pitcairn Field in Pennsylvania, she took the autogyro up to 15,000 feet, and later in the same day reached 18,415 feet.

Her Vega, registration NC7952, was coloured deep red and trimmed with gold. On 20 May 1932, she took off from Newfoundland in this distinctive machine and 15 hours and 30 minutes later landed in a field of cows near Londonderry in Northern Ireland. It was reported that she had killed one of the cows but she denied this, adding in characteristic fashion 'unless it died of fright'.

Amelia Earhart in August 1929 before the Women's Air Derby from Los Angeles to Cleveland. She flew a Lockheed Vega registration NC31E but overshot when landing at a refuelling airfield in Yuma and crashed the aircraft. *(John W. Underwood collection)*

Amelia Earhart with the borrowed Lockheed Vega 5A Executive, in which she established a new speed record of 184.17 mph on 22 November 1929. *(John W. Underwood collection)*

As the first woman to fly solo across the North Atlantic, Amelia's place in aviation history was assured, especially when aided by her husband's flair for publicity. He coined the nickname 'Lady Lindy' for her, as the female equivalent of Charles Lindbergh, to whom she bore some physical resemblance. Another of his names for her was 'First Lady of the Air'. Her fame continued to grow, to such an extent that she needed police protection in public from crowds of adoring fans. She designed a range of clothes similar to those she wore, and these were marketed as the 'Amelia Look'. She was awarded the civilian Distinguished Flying Cross.

The following year, Amelia bought another Vega, registration NC965Y, and had it painted red with silver trimmings. This was a version with more powerful engines. In August of that year she created another speed record by flying from Los Angeles in California to Newark in New Jersey. In the next year, she broke her own record. On 11–12 January 1935 she became the first person to fly from Hawaii to California, and indeed the first person to fly solo on this Pacific crossing. Meanwhile, she wrote her second autobiography, *The Fun of It*, and continued her hectic life of lecture tours and publicity. In those days, feats of aviation were still a novelty and she received shoals of fan mail as well as numerous awards. She became quite a close friend of Eleanor Roosevelt, the wife of the President. As a sideline, she earned additional money with 'first day covers' of postage stamps which commemorated her achievements.

Amelia's other accomplishments were a solo flight from Los Angeles to Mexico on 19–20 April 1935, and then a solo flight to Newark in New Jersey in the next month. But by then she was nearly thirty-eight years of age and could not expect her adventurous career to continue for many more years. There was only one additional record she intended to achieve, a flight round the world along a route which kept

Amelia Earhart posing with the Pitcairn PCA–2 autogyro, named Beech-Nut, which she enjoyed flying. *(John W. Underwood collection)*

Lockheed Vega C5 Special, registration NC-965-Y at Burbank in California. This was the machine in which Amelia Earhart became the first woman to fly from Hawaii to California, in January 1935, as well as the first person to fly solo over this stretch of the Pacific Ocean. *(John W. Underwood collection)*

Lockheed Vega C5 Special, which Amelia Earhart flew from Hawaii to California, on display at the 1936 aircraft show in Los Angeles. The first Douglas DC-3 commercial airliner, registration NC14988, is in the background. *(John W. Underwood collection)*

as close as possible to the Equator. This required a bigger and faster aircraft than her single-engined Vega. Aided by funds from research foundations, she bought in 1936 a twin-engined Lockheed 10-E Electra.

This aircraft was the product of some of the finest technology available at the time. The standard Electra had been in service with civil airlines since 1932 and was also employed by the US armed services for communication duties. It had a span of 55 feet, a length of 38 feet 7 inches and a height of 10 feet 1 inch. It was a low-wing monoplane of all-metal construction, with constant-speed propellers powered by two Pratt & Whitney R-985-13 Wasp Junior engines of 450 hp. But the standard Electra was modified considerably by the manufacturers to meet Amelia's requirements, being given the suffix 'E' for Earhart.

I am extremely grateful to the Lockheed Aeronautical Systems Company of Burbank, California, for providing details of this modified aircraft. Amelia's Electra 10-E, registration NR16020, was fitted with more powerful engines. These were Pratt & Whitney S3H1s, each providing a maximum 550 hp for one minute at 2,000 rpm. The standard machine was designed to carry ten passengers but the interior of the special Electra was adapted to take extra petrol tanks, bringing the total up to six tanks in the wings and six in the fuselage, with a capacity of 1,151 US gallons in all. This gave a theoretical range of 4,000 miles when flying in 'still air' conditions at a true airspeed of 145 mph and at an

Amelia Earhart's Lockheed 10-E Electra, registration NE16020, probably photographed in July 1936 when delivered to the Purdue Research Foundation. Most of the windows of the standard Lockheed 10 had been blanked out, and special tankage brought the total fuel capacity up to about 1,200 US gallons. *(Ralph Johnson collection)*

Amelia Earhart with her new Lockheed 10-E Electra registration NR16020. *(Bruce Robertson collection)*

altitude of 4,000 feet. But, as will be seen later, take-off with full fuel load was never achieved.

The machine was fitted with one of the first Sperry automatic pilots, later nicknamed 'George' by RAF pilots, which would relieve the physical strain on Amelia during flights which were expected to last for as long as eighteen hours during her new endeavour. A Cambridge fuel analyser monitored the air/fuel ratio from the exhaust gases, while a dial in the cockpit enabled Amelia to select the correct revolutions and boost for the most economical performance. An RCA loop aerial was fitted for direction-finding, of a type employed by the RAF in the same period. There was two-way voice and Morse radio equipment, Western Electric model 130C-HF transmitter and 20B receiver. Later, a gadget known as a 'sky-hook' was installed, designed to obtain in-flight samples of air-content for microscopic examination in laboratories. The machine

Amelia Earhart with the Pratt & Whitney S3N1 engine in the starboard wing of her 10-E Electra. *(John W. Underwood collection)*

was sometimes called a 'flying laboratory' but was christened *Lady Lindy* by George Putnam. It was coloured silver, with orange along the leading edges of the wings and on the tailplane.

It became apparent that Amelia could not attempt to fly across the Pacific Ocean without navigational assistance. Her knowledge of the art of navigation, especially celestial, was known to be little more than rudimentary. In her solo flights up to this time, her procedure had consisted mainly of flying compass course as accurately as possible and then trying to pick up visual pinpoints. When flying across oceans, she had always headed for large land masses which she was bound to reach eventually, provided there was sufficient fuel and no engine failure. For that reason, two men were asked to join Amelia's team for the long-distance sector across the Pacific Ocean.

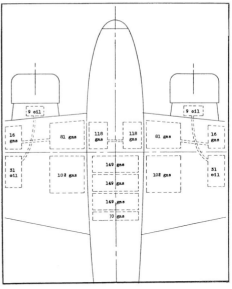

Gasoline and oil tank arrangement prepared for Amelia Earhart's Lockheed 10-E, drawn on 23 July 1936. This drawing gives totals of 1,151 gallons for gasoline and 80 gallons for oil. *(Lockheed Aircraft Corporation)*

The first was Captain Harry Manning, the commander of the US liner *President Roosevelt*. Amelia had sailed with him on her return to New York following her flight in the Fokker across the North Atlantic in 1928. He had tried to teach her the elements of celestial navigation but it has to be recorded that, like many other adventurous pilots, she found spherical trigonometry a tedious subject, best left to those who liked mathematical problems. Manning was asked to take leave of absence to accompany her on the first part of the Pacific crossing, when he would be the first navigator.

The second navigator was to be Frederick J. Noonan, born in Chicago in 1894 of Irish ancestry. He had served in the British Mercantile Marine during

Altitude	Time	r.p.m.	Manifold air pressure (boost)	Mixture	Fuel per hour
0–8,000ft	1hr	2,050	28½in Hg	0·078	100 US gal
8,000ft	3hr	1,900	28in Hg	0·073	60 US gal
8,000ft	3hr	1,800	26½in Hg	0·072	51 US gal
8,000ft	3hr	1,700	25in Hg	0·072	43 US gal
10,000ft	Thereafter	1,600	24in Hg	0·072	38 US gal

Fuel consumption for Pacific crossing (predicted by Lockheed).

the First World War and survived three occasions when his ships had been torpedoed. With many years at sea, Noonan had qualified as a master mariner, as had Harry Manning, and was thus an experienced astro-navigator with a good knowledge of the theoretical background of the subject matter.

In 1925 Noonan had left the sea to take up a position as a navigation instructor with Pan American Airways. He also had gained some experience as a pilot as well as an airport manager and inspector. Other experience had included flying as a navigator on the Martin 130 China Clipper, the four-engined flying boat which crossed the Pacific from California to Hong Kong. He had resigned from this company in 1937 with the intention of setting up his own navigation school. Favourable publicity for this project was likely to follow his part in Amelia's proposed flight. One problem was that, like Amelia's father, he indulged too much in alcohol, although this did not seem to affect his capacity for work. Moreover, he had married Mary B. Martinella on 27 March 1937 at Yuma in Arizona, which appeared to have had a steadying influence on his life.

Many of the facilities for navigation were good in the new Electra 10-E. A fair-sized navigation table was installed aft of the fuel tanks. There were chronometers beside the table, shock-mounted in rubber. These needed to be accurate to the second for the art of astro-navigation. All such navigation was carried out in Greenwich Mean Time, known in the USA as Greenwich Civil Time. There were also gauges for airspeed, altitude and air temperature, a drift recorder and a 'pelorus' or bearing compass. A bubble sextant was provided for measuring the altitude of the sun, moon, planets and stars. This was similar to the Mark IX sextant used in the RAF at the time. It provided an artificial horizon, thus eliminating the need for a sea horizon required by the marine sextant. Special hatches were fitted in the fuselage for taking these celestial observations, and later an astrodome was fitted.

However, there was one serious defect in the arrangements for navigation. There was poor intercommunication in the Electra 10-E, for the only way the navigator could reach the pilot was by crawling along a catwalk over the intervening fuel tanks. A simple system was devised whereby written messages could be clipped to the line of a bamboo fishing pole and passed between them. But one essential ingredient for successful long-distance flying, teamwork, was impaired by this inadequate method.

Another person who played a prominent part in Amelia's project was Albert Paul Mantz. Born in Almeda, California, he was thirty-three years of age in 1937 and acclaimed as one of the most skilful pilots in the Hollywood film industry. He was known as a 'stunt pilot' but he did not like this term and preferred to call himself a 'precision flyer'. This was probably more accurate, for he devoted himself to his career with remarkable intelligence and technical knowledge, reducing the risks involved to an acceptable minimum. He was still flying, apparently indestructibly, as recently as 1965 when he was tragically killed on location in Buttercup Valley during the filming of *Flight of the Phoenix*.

Paul Mantz's association with Amelia had lasted for several years, in terms of both business and friendship. When Amelia took delivery of her Electra 10-E, he curtailed his other activities to concentrate on preparations for her forthcoming flight. He made numerous flights with her in the new aircraft, which was considerably overweight with the extra fuel tanks. The 'operating weight' was 9,600lb, including all basic equipment, oil, crew and baggage, but without petrol. Then if, for example, 700 US gallons of petrol were loaded, the gross weight became 13,600lb, about 3,300lb more than the standard Electra 10-A. The machine thus required very careful handling, especially on take-off.

One problem which Mantz had to address was Amelia's lack of experience in handling twin-engined machines. He took her up on every possible day and devised a system of numbers and mnenomics for the cockpit drill. He was not completely happy with the result. Although Amelia learnt the drill and followed it precisely, she did not seem to have a natural aptitude for the controls. One habit he sought to correct was her tendency to jockey the throttles

Left to right: Harry Manning, Paul Mantz, Amelia Earhart. *(John W. Underwood collection)*

on take-off to correct the slight swings, instead of using the rudder once the machine had gathered sufficient speed. Nevertheless, a great deal of practice took place. Amelia also spent time in a Link Trainer on the ground, to improve her blind-flying techniques. It was arranged that Mantz would accompany her on the first part of the flight, from California to Hawaii, to act as co-pilot and correct any faults in her flying.

Another person who took an active part in the preparations for the flight was Vicomte Jacques de Sibour. He was a pilot who had flown in the First World War and had become an official with Standard Oil in New Jersey, which was to provide fuel for the entire flight. His wife Violette was also a pilot. She was one of the daughters of the American magnate Harry Gordon Selfridge, who had founded the department store of his name in Oxford Street, London. The couple were close friends of the Putnams and had had much experience of flying across Africa and India. Operating mainly from London, de Sibour arranged special fuel dumps at each planned and alternative landing place along the entire route. One of the facts I discovered at the Public Record Office is that the petrol was Stanavo Ethyl 87 octane, while the oil was Stanavo 120. The petrol was in drums containing 50 US gallons (44 Imperial gallons), bearing the name 'Amelia Earhart' in large red or white letters.

The planned route began in Oakland, California, and the first landing place was Wheeler Field in Honolulu, Hawaiian Islands. From there, it continued in a westerly direction, taking advantage of prevailing winds and timed to avoid poor climatic conditions in the countries to be crossed. Publicity was expertly arranged by George Putnam. In addition to her flying, Amelia was to carry boxes of philatelists' mail, to be posted at various stages en route. Quite astonishingly, she was also required to write a detailed diary and post each section to her husband, who would edit and then publish a book soon after her return. She performed this additional task with humour and verve, so that the results up to the time of her last take-off were indeed published, under the title *Last Flight*. Although the content reads something like a travelogue and seems rather naive in the more knowledgeable world of today, the book contains aeronautical details which are of value for research into her disappearance.

At about 16.30 hours local time on 17 March 1937, Amelia took off from Oakland on the first leg of her round-the-world flight, bound for Honolulu. Her crew consisted of Paul Mantz as co-pilot, with Harry Manning and Fred Noonan as navigators. The machine carried 947 US gallons of petrol for the flight of 2,400 miles. Somewhat surprisingly, this included 100 octane petrol, which was loaded into the forward wing tanks on one side. This higher octane gave slightly more power and longer combustion for take-offs, but thereafter 87 octane was used. The higher octane might have subjected the exhaust valves to overheating but replacement parts were provided for the Pratt & Whitney engines at landing places en route. Even with such a heavy load, the Electra lifted off after a fairly short run of 1,897 feet.

Six days before this date, Lockheed had sent a cable to Amelia in Oakland. These figures are reproduced here, and it will be seen later that they are extremely important in the analysis of her last flight. The average true airspeed for the Pacific crossing at these altitudes was 150 mph.

It was a smooth and uneventful flight to Honolulu. The loop aerial was used to help with the navigation during the final 100 miles to Wheeler Field. The winds were not unfavourable and the Electra arrived in 15 hours 47 minutes, giving an average groundspeed of 152 mph. It was a good start to the enterprise and a large crowd had gathered to welcome the successful crew. Amelia recorded that 'more than four hours of petrol remained'. This tallies closely with the figures provided by Lockheed, which indicated that 4 hours 21 minutes of flying time should have remained.

From Wheeler Field they flew to Luke Field in Ford Island, from where a concrete runway of 3,000 feet gave a longer take-off distance towards the waters of Pearl Harbor. Paul Mantz was to be left behind here, but Manning and Noonan were to continue as navigators. The next stop was to be the tiny American territory of Howland Island, 1,800 miles away. The aircraft was loaded with almost 900 US gallons of petrol, more than the flight required, but the weather ahead was uncertain and Amelia preferred to carry enough for about 19 hours of flight.

Disaster struck on take-off the following morning, when the aircraft was seen to swing to the right shortly before it reached take-off speed. The machine ground-looped and the starboard undercarriage collapsed. By some miracle, there was no fire and the occupants were not injured. Amelia said afterwards that she had reduced power on the port engine to correct the swing. This must have happened at a critical moment, when the aircraft was almost airborne. Some observers said that the swing was caused by a tyre blowing, but Amelia thought that the starboard shock-absorber (or oleo as it is normally called) might have given way. She wrote that when they were skidding to a halt her thoughts were, 'if we don't burn up, I want to go again'.

There was no alternative but to return to California, while the damaged *Lady Lindy* was crated and sent back to Lockheed for rebuilding. Among the items repaired were the starboard wing, the fuselage, the tail unit, both engine supports and the landing gear, at a total cost of about $14,000. To minimise danger on future take-offs, special shock struts were fitted to the undercarriage.

Cameramen at Oakland in California, taking photographs in March 1937 before the first attempt to fly round the world on an equatorial route. Left to right: Paul Mantz, Amelia Earhart, Harry Manning, Frederick Noonan. *(John W. Underwood collection)*

As a further safety precaution, equaliser lines were added to the cabin fuel tanks, in such a way that it became impossible for the centre of gravity to move outside safe limits.

This rebuilding was completed by 17 May 1937, about two months after the accident. By this time, climatic conditions around the world had undergone their seasonal changes and it was thought that the new attempt should be made in the reverse direction, towards the east. Harry Manning had returned to his Atlantic command, but Fred Noonan was prepared to accompany Amelia all the way around the world, instead of solely on the Pacific crossing.

Efforts were made to reduce the weight of the Electra in minor ways, and this included a decision which must have contributed to their deaths. The trailing aerial which enabled them to request bearings on 500 kilohertz, the frequency on which these were normally transmitted from ground stations, was removed. Amelia disliked having to wind in and out an aerial of 250 feet, and neither she nor Noonan was adept at Morse code signalling. Mantz was appalled when he heard later of this decision. In my recollection, however, it was characteristic of the attitude to air navigation at the time. When I first joined the RAFVR in 1939, navigators who resorted to radio bearings were considered deficient in their jobs, while the bearings themselves were often judged to be unreliable and potentially dangerous. Meticulous dead-reckoning, accurate map-reading and astro-navigation were regarded as the hallmarks of good navigation in those days.

On 20 May 1937, three days after the rebuilt Electra was delivered, Amelia and Noonan took off from Oakland on the new attempt to fly around the world. The first legs were via Tucson and New Orleans to Miami, but they did not arrive there until 23 May. There was a small fire in the port engine at Tucson and minor repairs were required. Then, at 0550 hours local time on 1 June, they took off for San Juan in the American island of Puerto Rico, where they arrived without incident. They reached Carapito in Venezuela on the following day, and spent the night there. Then they flew to Paramaribo in Dutch Guinea, where they spent another night. The next day involved a flight to Fortaleza in Brazil, where the following day was spent servicing the engines and checking the instruments. On 6 June, they flew to Natal in Brazil. The aircraft was closely inspected by customs officials every time they landed, as well as fumigated to destroy any insects. The most difficult parts of the venture were still ahead of them.

The flight across the South Atlantic, a distance of about 1,900 miles, was made on 7 June. There was an odd incident on this part of the project. They were headed for Dakar in Senegal, part of French West Africa, but evidently

The damaged Lockheed 10-E Electra at Luke Field in Ford Island, Hawaii, after ground-looping on take-off for Howland Island on 19 March 1937. It was shipped back to Lockheed for extensive repairs. (John W. Underwood collection)

The rebuilt 10-E Electra, fitted with an astrodome in front of the radio mast. *(John W. Underwood collection)*

arrived on the coast about 20 miles to the north of the promontory on which the port is situated. It was clear to Noonan that they were to the north of Dakar, for the direction of the coast ran to the north-north-east, whereas the coast to the south of the port ran in a south-south-easterly direction. However, Amelia refused to fly the course he gave her and instead flew in the other direction. Eventually they landed at St Louis in Senegal, 163 miles from their destination. Of course, Amelia had to admit her mistake. Although she was fulsome in her praise of Noonan and his abilities in the notes she sent to her husband, it was clear she had no great faith in air navigation and preferred to follow her instincts. Perhaps the poor communication in the Electra was a factor in her wrong decision, but the error was a bad omen for the remainder of their flight.

The journey across Africa lasted four days. On 10 June they flew to Gao in French West Africa, on the River Niger. The next day brought a flight to Port Lamy in French Chad, and on 12 June they reached El Fasher in Anglo-Egyptian Sudan. Navigation across this territory proved somewhat difficult, for the country had been inadequately mapped, and Noonan used sun shots to aid his calculations. On the following day, they flew to Massawa in Italian Eritrea, with a brief stay in Khartoum en route. Then followed a short hop down the coast to Assab in Eritrea, near the entrance to the Red Sea.

The flight of about 1,950 miles to Karachi in India took place on 15 June. Owing to political unrest, they were not permitted to fly over any part of the Arabian peninsula other than Aden, and the flight was made in one long hop. It was accomplished without any difficulty, and they were very pleased to be welcomed by Jacques and Violette de Sibour and to have their Electra serviced by a combination of Imperial Airways and the obliging RAF. On arrival in India and from that time onwards, Amelia and Noonan were besieged by eager newspaper reporters. Some of these wrote for women's pages but others were air correspondents who were more interested in technical details. It will be seen later that some of these technical reports are of value in establishing the fate of the aircraft and its occupants.

On 17 June they flew on to Dum-Dum, near Calcutta, where they landed after a torrential downpour, for they had met the monsoon. However, they refuelled and took off for Akyab in Burma, flying at low altitude to keep under the dangerous clouds. They attempted to reach Rangoon on 19 June but the monsoon rains beat on the Electra with such violence that they were forced to turn back to Akyab, where they found that paint had been stripped off the leading edges of the wings.

The weather was little better on the following day, but they pressed on to Rangoon and spent the night there. They were very relieved when they flew clear of the monsoon on the next day and reached Singapore, after refuelling at Bangkok. Following an overnight stop, they continued to Bandoeng in Java, part of the Dutch East Indies, where the Electra developed some sort of instrument fault which Amelia did not specify in her notes. The engines were also serviced. These repairs delayed them for a day, but the instrument trouble recurred on the flight to Surabaya in east Java on 24 June. At this point in her account, Amelia mentions 'long-distance flying instruments'. It seems possible that the trouble occurred in the gas analyser, which had two dials and had required attention at Dakar after the flight over the South Atlantic. Alternatively, there may have been an electrical fault in the engine instrument panel, or even something wrong with the directional gyro. Whatever it was, Amelia decided to fly back to Bandoeng, where there were facilities for repair.

These repairs caused some delays, and in this period Amelia suffered from enteritis, a debilitating illness which often afflicted travellers in this tropical region. It was not until 27 June that they were able to leave Bandoeng for Koepang in the Dutch island of Timor, from where they continued to Port Darwin in Australia. Here their instruments were checked by the Royal Australian Air Force and Amelia decided to reduce weight further by sending their parachutes home to America, judging that these would be of no use over the Pacific.

On 29 June, they flew to Lae in New Guinea, a territory which at the time was mandated to Australia. The flight of about 1,200 miles was completed in 7 hours 43 minutes against headwinds and around towering cumulus clouds. By this time, they had flown about 22,000 miles since leaving Oakland on 20 May.

Both Amelia and Noonan must have been feeling extremely tired. It had been a gruelling experience for them, beset with problems and with inadequate relaxation, but they still had to face the greatest test of all, crossing the vast Pacific Ocean.

Lae airfield was at the end of the Markham river, overlooking Huon Gulf. It consisted of a grass runway cut out of the jungle in a north-west to south-east direction, 150 feet wide and 3,000 feet long, ending on a cliff which dropped 20 feet to the sea below. Beyond that was their next objective, Howland Island, 2,556 miles away. This was only two miles long and half a mile wide, about 20 feet above sea level at its highest point. The Americans had built an airstrip on it, partly to receive the Electra, and refuelling facilities had been provided.

Two vessels were detached from the American base at Honolulu to provide assistance with the flight to Howland Island. One was the ocean-going and armed tug USS *Ontario*, which was ordered to 'stand to' halfway along the route. The other was the US Coast Guard cutter *Itasca*, 1,975 tons, which was positioned near Howland Island to take and transmit radio bearings, as well as to provide a visual signal by making smoke. The Americans in California were hoping to welcome their heroine on Independence Day, 4 July, for the Electra would gain a day when crossing the International Date Line.

Amelia and Noonan spent 30 June preparing for their flight, waiting for clear skies for astro shots and favourable winds to help them on their way. Noonan also needed to obtain a time signal for his chronometers, to ensure that they were accurate to the second. The airfield was run by Guinea Airways, and the manager Eric Chaters arranged a thorough check of the Electra, servicing the engines and instruments. Amelia insisted on reducing the weight further in every possible way, unloading all surplus equipment and baggage. According to one witness, even the survival kit was taken off.

Several witnesses stated that Noonan began drinking heavily. No doubt some ebullient and hospitable Australians were more than ready to provide him with cheerful company. But according to the best evidence he drank whisky only during the evening of 30 June, when Amelia was away at a dinner party. It seems that he refrained from drinking during the evening before the day of take-off, when he and Amelia were making their final preparations.

At 1000 hours local time, Amelia took off from Lae for Howland Island. According to eyewitnesses, the Electra lifted off sluggishly when about 100 feet from the end of the grass runway, sank down towards the sea and then began a very slow climb to the east. In her final letter to her husband, Amelia had written that it was 'loaded to capacity'. The last words which reached him were: 'Not much more than a month ago, I was on the other side of the Pacific, looking westward. This evening I looked eastward over the Pacific. In the fast-moving days which have intervened the whole width of the world has passed behind me – except this broad ocean. I shall be glad when we have the hazards of its navigation behind us.'

One of the most interesting aspects of any enquiry into the disappearance of Amelia Earhart is that there were several voice-to-voice transmissions from her before the Electra was lost. The exact content of some of these messages has been the subject of some dispute but, even allowing for differences in records, they provide important clues to the fate of the aircraft and its passengers.

Throughout her world flight Amelia gave messages every half-hour as a matter of routine, using her call-sign KHAQQ, but not knowing with any certainty whether she could be heard. The crystals available for the radio set installed in the Electra gave her the facility of calling on 6,210 Hz, which was the frequency normally used during daylight hours, and on 3,105 Hz, which was the night frequency. It is difficult to establish the exact range of these medium-frequency transmissions. The equipment was considered to have a range of up to 400 miles, but transmissions were better over sea than land. Moreover, there is the phenomenon of 'skip distance', when sky waves bounce off the layer of ionised gases round the earth's atmosphere, known as the 'Heaviside Layer'. These give much longer ranges than the ground waves, especially at night. Even in those days, radio operators could quote instances of receiving freak messages, sometimes from thousands of miles away.

It is simpler to relate Amelia's messages in terms of GMT, since she took off from Lae for Howland Island at precisely 0000 hours GMT (1000 hours local time) on 2 July 1937 and then flew through a number of time zones. Indeed it seems obvious that Amelia chose this time to take off deliberately, so that she could check their progress easily, knowing in advance the calculated times for each stage of the flight. Her ETA at Howland Island was 1800 hours GMT, which was only a few minutes after sunrise on arrival.

The early part of the flight was in daylight, during which they must have passed over several islands which gave visual pinpoints for the plotting chart. The night flight took place mainly over the open sea, when Noonan would have expected to use astro-navigation on the plentiful stars and planets he could select, provided the sky was clear enough.

At Lae, the radio operator heard Amelia very clearly during the first hours of the flight. She reported at one stage that she could see clouds ahead and was reducing altitude from 10,000 feet. At 0720 hours GMT, when she would still have been flying in daylight, she gave the only positive position report of the

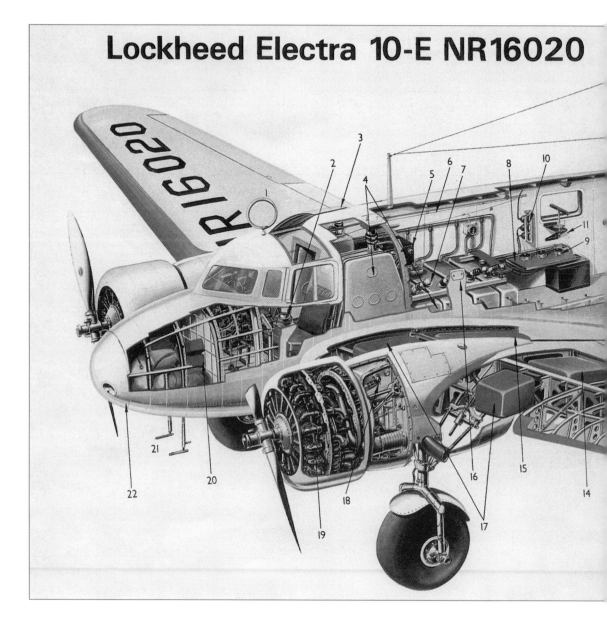

Lockheed Electra 10-E NR16020

flight. This was 04° 33' South 159° 06' West, which is about 20 miles south-west of the Nukumanu Islands. This position is significant for two reasons. The first is that she had flown about 850 miles, so that radio conditions must have been excellent at the time. Secondly, the Electra was making an average groundspeed of only about 120 mph. Even though this takes into account her slow climb in the heavily laden machine, it indicates that they were already experiencing headwinds. The forecast wind had been very light, only 12 mph from the south-east. But an examination of the reported winds for the day at the National Meteorological Archive at Bracknell shows that the wind for the day

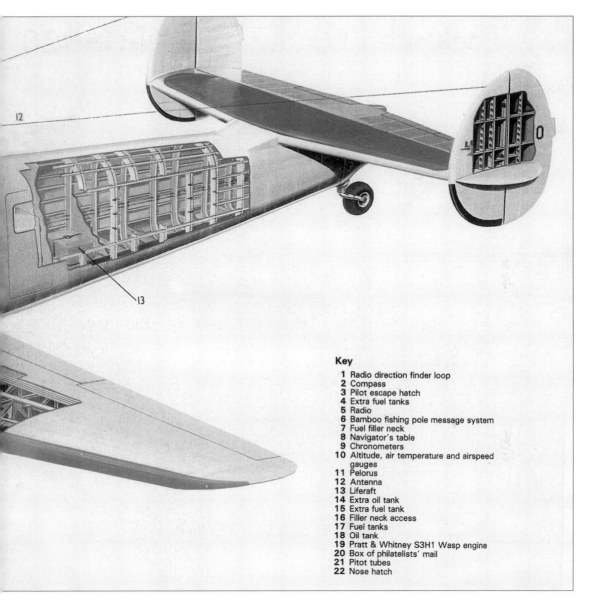

Key
1 Radio direction finder loop
2 Compass
3 Pilot escape hatch
4 Extra fuel tanks
5 Radio
6 Bamboo fishing pole message system
7 Fuel filler neck
8 Navigator's table
9 Chronometers
10 Altitude, air temperature and airspeed gauges
11 Pelorus
12 Antenna
13 Liferaft
14 Extra oil tank
15 Extra fuel tank
16 Filler neck access
17 Fuel tanks
18 Oil tank
19 Pratt & Whitney S3H1 Wasp engine
20 Box of philatelists' mail
21 Pitot tubes
22 Nose hatch

was about 25 mph from due east at medium height. Although this was recorded further east along her track, at Nauru Island (a territory administered jointly by Britain, Australia and New Zealand), it indicates that there was a stronger headwind than forecast.

Amelia must have flown over Nauru at night, at about 1100 hours GMT. The radio operator there picked up some transmissions which seemed to be Amelia's voice, but he had difficulty in making out the content. There are varying reports of what he heard, including 'land in sight', 'a ship in sight' and 'lights ahead'. The American tug USS *Ontario* was well to the south of Nauru Island and her radio operator heard nothing. It seems most probable that Amelia saw the lights of the phosphate workings on Nauru Island, for she had been notified in advance of these.

From Nauru, the route of the Electra crossed over the British Gilbert Islands, a long string lying athwart its track, but it seems that the authorities there had not been asked to assist in any way. I could find nothing in the records of these islands in relation to Amelia Earhart in the Public Record Office. Nevertheless, it seems probable that Amelia and Noonan were able to make a visual pinpoint of their position over the islands and at that stage knew exactly where they were.

Noonan must have been busy taking astro shots throughout the night. This method is seldom used nowadays, when satellites give precise ground positions to aircraft, surface craft and even land vehicles. In 1937 and throughout the Second World War, the standard method was to use a sextant to obtain the angle between the horizon and the body in the sky, noting the time to the exact second. Using tables, the navigator could then obtain a position line on his chart at right angles to the direction (or azimuth) of the body. Three of these position lines were obtained from different bodies in fairly quick succession. The first two were then transferred along the aircraft's track in accordance with groundspeed and time, so that the intersection of the three lines then gave a reasonably accurate ground position, or 'fix'.

This method may seem complicated, but with practice a trained astro-navigator could expect his calculated 'fix' to be within about three miles of the

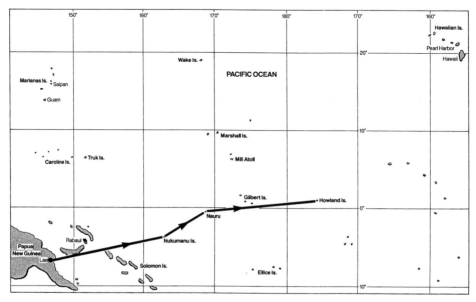

Probable route from Lae to Howland Island on 2 July 1937, taking advantage of visual pinpoints from islands.

true position, provided the sky was fairly clear and there was not too much turbulence. During the day, however, only the sun was available to give a single position line, so that the position of the aircraft along this line was not known with any accuracy unless other methods, such as radio bearings, were available to give further position lines.

The most dramatic calls from Amelia were picked up by the US Coast Guard cutter *Itasca*, positioned near Howland Island specifically to assist in the last stages of the navigation. The seamen noted that there were ominous dark clouds to the north-west of their vessel, which did not augur well for the arrival of the Electra. Visibility was not as good as had been hoped, so that the occupants of the aircraft would not have been able to see the smoke from afar when flying at lower level beneath the cloud base.

There were two radio operators on duty and their records differ somewhat with regard to exact content of the messages. At 1744 hours GMT, only 16 minutes before the Electra was due to arrive, they heard her call 'Bearing on 3105 – on hour – will whistle in mike.' A minute later she said 'About 200 miles out. Approximately. Whistling now.' Significantly, 1745 hours was the time of sunrise over the island, but sunrise could not yet be seen from the Electra. Amelia seems to have been emphasising their lateness and was probably starting to get worried. The position of the Electra must have been plotted by Noonan on his chart from a combination of dead-reckoning and a succession of astro fixes during the night.

At 1815 hours GMT, Amelia was heard to ask for a bearing on her aircraft and to give her position as 'about 100 miles out'. The Electra could not have flown 100 miles in the 30 minutes since her last message, even allowing for any 'rounding' of distances. This revision of position provides a very important clue to the ultimate fate of the machine and its occupants. It evidently occurred as a result of a 'sunrise position line' calculated by Noonan at about 1755 hours GMT. This was done without using the sextant but simply by noting the exact time the 'upper limb' of the sun appeared on the sea horizon. In those latitudes and at that time of year, this is usually seen as a sudden and brilliant flash of light. The Electra was flying directly towards it. In anticipation, Noonan had probably moved forward over the fuel tanks with one of his chronometers.

By comparing this time with the known time of sunrise at Howland Island, it was easy for Noonan to convert time into distance. The result seems to have been 160 nautical miles travelling distance to the island. Taking into account the probable groundspeed of the Electra, this distance would have been reduced to 'about 100 miles' at the time Amelia sent her message at 1815 hours GMT.

This sunrise position method of checking longitude was not normally used by air navigators but was common among marine navigators. Certainly Noonan would have been familiar with the method as a qualified master navigator and must have used it on occasions when on board ship. It was the only method he could have employed in the Electra at this time, for the stars and planets had faded from the sky. But it did contain an inherent danger when taken from the air, as will be seen shortly.

At 1912 hours GMT, Amelia called 'We must be on you now but cannot see you. But gas is running low. Been unable to reach you by radio. We are flying at 1,000 feet.' According to one of the two operators, this message included 'Running out of gas, only half an hour left.' It is interesting to note that 1912 hours was the revised ETA at Howland Island which Noonan had calculated, provided he had used the sunrise method of checking longitude and had assumed that there were no errors in his calculations. Meanwhile the fuel gauges in the Electra would not have enabled Amelia to determine exactly how much fuel remained in the tanks, but she would have known that they were almost exhausted.

At 1929 hours GMT, the operators in *Itasca* heard Amelia say 'We are circling but cannot hear you. Go ahead on 7,500 either now or on the schedule time on half hour.' This message came through at maximum strength. Unfortunately 7,500 kHz was not a frequency on which bearings of the Electra could be taken. The American seamen expected to take bearings on 500 kHz, but did not know that the trailing aerial for this frequency had been removed from the aircraft. It seems that Amelia was unable to make out any of the voice-to-voice transmissions sent to her, at least up to this stage in the flight.

Then, at 2014 hours GMT, Amelia sent her last message: 'We are on line of position 157 to 337. Will repeat this message on 6,210 kcs. Wait, listening on 6,210 kcs. We are running north and south.' This message came through at maximum strength. According to one of the operators, her voice was considered 'broken and frenzied'. No further messages from her were heard.

This 'line of position' has caused some confusion among researchers, but an official at the Royal Greenwich Observatory has confirmed to me that it was that derived from sunrise and could have been taken from the Electra at about 1755 hours GMT. It is possible that Noonan might have used a technique employed by marine navigators, probably for a century or more. It was also known to air navigators. The method was recorded by Francis Chichester who, before achieving fame as a round-the-world yachtsman, was a highly experienced aviator and astro-navigator.

Chichester described the procedure in his book *Astro-Navigation* and called it 'Running Down a Position Line'. When trying to find a small island in daylight, with only the sun to provide a position line, the navigator did not head straight for it, since a slight error in calculations might cause him to pass either left or right without seeing it. Instead, he aimed for one side or the other, sufficiently far to know which side he was on. When nearing the island, he took an astro shot with his sextant. This gave a position line, which he transferred along the track on his chart until it cut through the island and gave a turning point. His estimated ground speed gave the ETA at this turning point. He then flew along this transferred position line until he could see the island. Chichester quoted an example in 1931 when he used this technique while flying in a Moth seaplane across the Pacific.

It is certain that Noonan knew of this technique, but far less certain that he was able to use it on his last flight. A simple sketch shows the method he might have employed, but by using the *sunrise* position line instead of an astro shot. But it is extremely unlikely that Amelia would have agreed to fly a dog-leg to Howland Island, with her limited appreciation of navigational techniques and in the knowledge that the fuel was running very low. Instead, the Electra was probably aiming direct for Howland Island.

If this reasoning is correct, it is possible to suggest what went wrong. Marine navigators used the sunrise position line, without a sextant but by simply

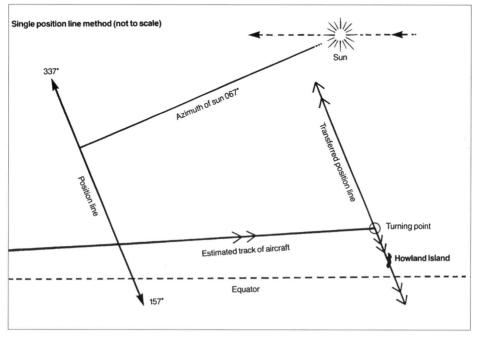

The method of finding a small island on the ocean by obtaining a single position line and then transferring it along the track in order to fly a dogleg.

noting the time. The sea was their horizon and the sextant angle was nil. But the higher one flies, the earlier one sees the sun rise over the horizon, and a correction known as 'dip' is required. At 1,000 feet, this correction is about 31 miles, at 2,000 feet it is 44 miles and at 5,000 feet it is about 70 miles. If the correction was not made, Noonan would have calculated that the Electra was nearer Howland Island than was the case.

One might expect Noonan to have remembered the need for this 'dip' correction but he was more used to the technique as a marine navigator than an air navigator. Moreover, he had been working intensively for eighteen hours without a break. His brain is almost certain to have become dulled at this stage. It seems probable that Amelia's message at 1745 hours GMT that they were '200 miles out' was correct, whereas the message at 1815 hours GMT that they were '100 miles out' was incorrect. Thus they were flying north and south along a position line which was at least 31 miles west of Howland Island.

The question of the remaining fuel in the Electra at the time of Amelia's last message at 2014 hours GMT should be considered, and here there are some important clues in British records. It will be appreciated that in order to fly over territory which was part of the British Commonwealth, Amelia had first to obtain the necessary authority. Original correspondence on this subject is available at the Public Record Office. On 13 February 1937, Amelia wrote to Lieutenant-Colonel Sir Francis Shelmerdine, the Director of Civil Aviation. It may be worth quoting this letter in full:

My dear Sir Francis,

At the suggestion of Jacques de Sibour, good friend of Mr Putnam's and mine, I am venturing this letter. It supplements a radiogram sent today to de Sibour, a copy of which I attach.

In that cable, I tried to outline pertinent facts of the contemplated flight. The State Department here has generously co-operated throughout and apparently is encountering no difficulty in securing necessary permissions. However, I am informed this morning that permissions involving Arabia have not yet been received.

You will understand, of course, that the plane has an international licence and in all matters pertaining to the proposed flight has the thorough approval of the United States Department of Commerce. Only with that approval could the State Department act.

So far as the ship is concerned, your interest is no doubt in its fuel tankage, i.e. 1,150 gallons. Such amount provides a maximum range of more than 4,000 miles.

My longest hops over the Pacific are about 2,500 miles – at which time I shall carry *probably 1,000 gallons of gasoline* [my italics]. So, actually before reaching the territory there will have been take-offs with that amount of gasoline.

Beyond the Pacific there will be no necessity for take-offs involving much more than 700 gallons of gas. Even at pretty generous cruising speed that would give me 2,000 miles cruising range. For your information, I have already made numerous take-offs with more than 700 gallons on board, following them up with extensive flights.

The day before yesterday, for instance, I flew from St Louis to New York, a distance of more than 900 miles, averaging 197 miles an hour, without high favouring winds. The gas consumption is working out very satisfactorily. Apparently the consumption, on normal cruising at 65 per cent power output, will not exceed 25 gallons per hour per engine.

By actual thorough-going test the ship can remain aloft on one engine on normal loads. As I have fuel dump valves in all but one tank it is possible to lighten the load very quickly.

I presume that you will know just what has been done in connection with the applications made by the State Department for permission. I have, by the way, informed the Department that I am taking up this general matter with you, supplementing whatever they have done – course entirely agreeable.

This letter then is to request such permission as may be necessary and any special instruction and guidance which it is in order that I should receive.

I am deeply grateful for your interest and such co-operation as you may be able to extend.

Sincerely yours,
Amelia Earhart

The accompanying telegram was also dated 13 February 1937, sent by George Putman to Jacques de Sibour at his telegraphic address of Stanair, London. It is repeated here in full, giving normal punctuation for clarity.

De Sibour only. Permission thus far not received by State Department is Arabia. Amelia writing Shelmerdine via steamer *Hansa* sailing tomorrow. Grateful for his co-operation, hopeful he can start action pending letter's receipt. You know route Lockheed Electra, two H Wasp engines larger than regular equipment, capable of staying aloft on one with normal load.

Designed gross load 10,500lb. Maximum gross load on present journey outside of Pacific hop within 40 per cent overload, with cruising range 2,000 miles. All tanks have dump valves. Total tanks 1,150 gallons but maximum contemplated outside Pacific is 700 gallons. Fuel consumption normal cruising per hour by weight 310lb. Test take-offs with 850 gallons have been made and with 1,000 will be made. Two-way radio, voice and telegraph, automatic pilot. Has NR licence, full official approval. Probably solo, though possibly accompanied navigator Harry Manning. Both recently inoculated typhoid, smallpox. Carrying certificates, no firearms or motion-picture equipment.

Putnam

In a cordial reply to Amelia, dated 5 March 1937, Sir Francis Shelmerdine gave permission for the flight. He had obtained approval from the Foreign Secretary, Sir Anthony Eden, with the proviso that Aden was to be the only landing place in the flight over Arabia. Sir Francis reminded Amelia that they had met on the yacht *Evadne* belonging to the aviation manufacturer Richard Fairey.

The amount of fuel located at landing points is also included in these records. At Lae it was 700 US gallons of Stanavo Ethyl 87 octane, with 70 US gallons of oil. When the direction of the flight was changed, after the crash on take-off at Luke Field in Hawaii, authority was given for the new arrangement. The amount of petrol at Lae was increased to 800 US gallons.

It is clear from these records that Amelia intended to carry no more than 1,000 US gallons on her 'Pacific hop' and was practising take-offs with up to that amount. This agrees with her flight from California to Honolulu when she carried 947 gallons, as well as her intended flight from Honolulu to Howland Island, when she intended to take off with about 900 gallons but crashed.

Of course, it may be argued that when she reached Lae on 29 June 1937, she changed her mind and decided to take off from the grass runway with a grossly overloaded aircraft containing 1,150 US gallons. But there were authoritative witnesses who confirmed that she stuck to her original plans. These were the reporters and air correspondents who were present at Lae. Their evidence can be found in the British Museum Newspaper Library at Colindale in North London. The most detailed report was written by the air correspondent of the very responsible *Daily Telegraph* of Sydney in Australia, who obtained his information from Noonan and reported it on 5 July. The Electra was loaded with a total of 950 US gallons. Noonan also stated that the machine was overloaded to the extent of two tons. The normal gross take-off weight of the Electra was 10,300lb.

Amelia Earhart – Final Moments
by Charles J. Thompson GAva, ASAA, GMA, EAA

The Lockheed 10-E near Howland Island, with its fuel exhausted and the port engine stopped, before coming down in the sea.

The weight of take-off at Lae with 950 US gallons was just over 14,300lb, as near as can be calculated. Two US tons are 4,000lb. This record tallies exactly.

So precise were the details recorded by the Australian air correspondent that other items mentioned taken on board the Electra were iced water, hot coffee, hot tomato soup, sandwiches, four hard-boiled eggs and three cakes of plain chocolate.

According to the predicted figures from Lockheed, as illustrated on p. 9, 950 US gallons gave the Electra an endurance of 20 hours 13 minutes. However, the weight of the machine had been reduced slightly after these figures were compiled, and a slightly longer endurance must have resulted. Amelia's last desperate message was received 20 hours 25 minutes after take-off from Lae. It is clear that she must have come down in the sea only a few minutes later, somewhere near Howland Island.

It may seem extraordinary that so small a safety margin was allowed for the flight, but this was typical of the risks that attended such long-distance flights in those days. Amelia must have remembered her disastrous attempt at take-off with about 900 US gallons of petrol from Luke Field in Hawaii, and balanced the danger of take-off with a grossly overladen aircraft with the danger of running out of fuel. In the earlier flight, from California to Honolulu, she had taken off with 947 gallons of fuel and landed with over four hours remaining, having flown 2,400 miles. The flight from Lae to Howland Island was only 150 miles longer and the reserve of fuel may have seemed adequate. But, unlike the flight to Honolulu, they were beaten by adverse winds, poor weather in the last part of the flight, and inadequate radio direction-finding facilities.

Within a few hours of Amelia's last message the captain of the cutter *Itasca*, Commander Walter K. Thompson, headed his vessel to the north-west, for he reasoned that the Electra was most likely to have come down somewhere beneath the storm clouds in that direction. At this stage in aviation development, it was believed that all-metal aircraft could float for quite a long time, provided the fuel tanks were empty. This belief was dispelled during the Second World War, for it was found that they sank within a minute or two. It was also believed that the Electra had on board a rubber dinghy equipped with lifebelts, flares, Very pistol, emergency rations and even a signal kite. It was hoped that, at the very least, Amelia and Noonan would be able to clamber into this and were awaiting rescue. Unfortunately, it seems probable that this emergency equipment was off-loaded at Lae as part of the effort to reduce weight.

The US Navy put into operation a large search, with Consolidated Catalinas as well as surface vessels. Destroyers, minesweepers, and even a battleship with reconnaissance aircraft were diverted to the area. The New Zealand cruiser HMS

Achilles heard messages from KHAQQ which included 'Quite down, but radio still working'. Unfortunately the log of his cruiser is not in the Public Record Office. It seems probable that this was one of the many radio hoaxes sent out by malicious people after the Electra was reported missing.

These hoax messages are not worthy of repeating here, but it is sufficient to say that some were given credence at the time. For the most part, they implied that Electra was floating somewhere but still able to transmit. Paul Mantz, Amelia's technical adviser, pointed out that there was no hand-crank mechanism for electricity in the aircraft and that transmission was impossible unless the Electra was on a reef somewhere with an engine ticking over. Nevertheless, the hoaxes resulted in the *Itasca* being ordered away from its area of search to examine the sea south of Howland Island.

George Putnam seized on some of these hoax messages as giving evidence of survival and made a nuisance of himself with the authorities. A spirit medium who was a friend of Amelia told Putnam that his wife was still alive in the floating Electra, while Noonan was injured. Another medium announced that she was in communication with Amelia, who was dead and lying in 12 feet of water, having jumped out by parachute. Mantz pointed out that the parachutes had been left behind in Darwin.

An immense area of the ocean was searched, covering a radius of about 700 miles from Howland Island. There was a flurry of excitement when flares were believed seen, but these proved to be a shower of meteors. An aircraft carrier arrived to help. The search was reported to have involved ten ships, 102 aircraft and 3,000 men, and to have cost $3 million. Nothing whatsoever was found.

There have been persistent rumours and many conspiracy theories since that date, some of them resting on the belief that Amelia was on a spy mission and had been captured by the Japanese. To some extent, these were prompted by a film which appeared in 1943, entitled *Flight to Freedom*. Obviously based on Amelia's last flight, a couple were sent on a disguised spying flight across the Pacific, which they accomplished but had to remain incognito. They lived happily together ever after. In 1949, Amelia's mother expressed the belief that her daughter was on a secret mission, although Eleanor Roosevelt said that her husband had never hinted there was anything secret about the flight.

All the available evidence from public records indicates that the Electra came down somewhere to the west of Howland Island, probably within about 30 miles. The north-west appears to have been the most likely direction, since Amelia was flying at 1,000 feet and thus indicating that they were below cloud. But we do not know how far they flew to the north or to the south along the position line 157 to 337 degrees, thus widening the area of possibility. There is also the likelihood that they spent some of their remaining minutes chasing shadows thrown on the sea by the clouds, which gave the impression of low-lying islands. When flying in a Dakota over the South China Sea in that latitude soon after the end of the war, I recollect seeing a puzzling shape in the sea on our starboard bow, which might have been such a shadow. We were curious enough to alter course towards it, to discover that it was a very small atoll on the eastern fringe of the Paracel Islands.

What happened when they were forced to ditch in the sea can only be a matter of conjecture. According to Commander Thompson of the *Itasca*, the sea was very rough when he sailed to the north-west, with waves of up to 6 feet whipped up by the strong wind from the east. The captain of a Catalina from Honolulu which arrived on the scene soon afterwards was astonished to experience snow showers and severe icing at the Equator. Paul Mantz, who remained consistently level-headed after the tragedy became known, gave his opinion in the light of his knowledge of Amelia's flying capabilities. He said that Noonan must have missed the island and the Electra must have come down in the sea. Then he suggested two possibilities. One was that Amelia tried to

Dana Timmer of Howland Landing Ltd in Nevada, the organiser of the underwater search for Amelia Earhart's Lockheed 10-E in the Pacific, photographed at the headquarters of Carlton-Central Television in Portman Square, London, on 16 July 2001. *(Author's collection)*

The Williamson and Associates SM 30 sidescan sonar carried by the survey vessel *June T. (Dana Timmer)*

land too high above the water, so that the Electra stalled and killed both of them. The other was that, if the sea was very rough, she might have made a bad judgement and flown into a heavy roller, with a similar result.

Amelia always thought that her end might come in such a way. She wrote her own epitaph several years before her last flight: 'Hooray for the last great adventure! I wish I had won, but it was worth while anyway.'

My original article on this subject was written in collaboration with Flight Lieutenant Ernest Schofield DFC, another ex-RAF navigation instructor who also flew on some long-range special missions using astro-navigation techniques. This was picked up and utilised by an American team in an underwater hunt for Amelia Earhart's Lockheed 10-E.

The first part of this hunt took place in November and December 1999. It was organised by Howland Landing Ltd, Williamson & Associates Inc. and Guy Zacone Productions, in co-operation with International Bridge Corporation and its survey vessel *June T*. After leaving the Marshall Islands in the Pacific, the ship was on site near Howland Island for more than 30 days and surveyed some 600 miles of ocean bottom, digitally mapping a hitherto unknown area. Using

The survey vessel *June T* of about 900 tons. She was built as an oil tanker. *(Dana Timmer)*

Williamson & Associates' SM 30 sidescan sonar tethered to more than five miles of cable, the search reached depths down as far as 18,000 feet.

The average depth of the sea bottom in the area is probably about 17,000 feet. It is desert-like, flat and uncluttered with objects. A number of potential targets were logged by specialists at Williamson's offices in Seattle. After being computer-enhanced, they can be examined by remote-operated vehicles (ROVs) capable of video and still imaging. However, only about half the potential area has been surveyed and it is anticipated that the remainder will be covered on a future expedition. This is being put together by the manager of Howland Landing Ltd, Dana Timmer. Such projects are very expensive and require private funds as well as a great deal of organisation.

CHAPTER TWO

Amy Johnson

Amy Johnson baled out of her aircraft and was drowned in the Thames Estuary on 5 January 1941. Rumours and mysteries have surrounded her death since that date, as is usually the case when a famous person loses his or her life and the circumstances have not been fully explained. When the editor of the well-known aviation magazine *Aeroplane Monthly*, Richard Riding, asked me some years ago to carry out another investigation into this tragedy, my first reaction was to assume that the circumstances had been examined so often that nothing more could be discovered. In the event, however, I found that there are several significant facts available in public records which other researchers appeared to have overlooked. Indeed, it seems to me that these additional records indicate quite clearly that she baled out over the Thames Estuary and how she lost her life.

Amy Johnson was born on 1 July 1903 at Kingston-upon-Hull. She was the eldest daughter of John William Johnson, a wealthy herring importer, and his wife Amy. After attending secondary school, the young Amy went to the University of Sheffield and graduated with a BA in Economics. However, she was unable to find suitable employment for a person with her qualifications and eventually took a position as a secretary with a firm of solicitors in the City of London. Her hobbies were flying and mechanical engineering, which were rather unusual for a young lady of those days, and she spent much of her time in the London Aeroplane Club at Edgware. She became the first woman in Britain to be awarded the Air Ministry's ground engineering licence, and also qualified as a pilot and navigator.

On 5 May 1930, while still an inexperienced pilot, she took off in an attempt to break the light aeroplane record for a solo flight to Australia. The project was partly inspired by her father, who was proud of his adventurous daughter, and she adopted his company's trademark of 'Jason' as the name of her de Havilland DH60G Moth letters G-AAAH. She did not break the record but arrived at Port Darwin on 24 May and then flew on to Brisbane, where weariness caused her to damage the undercarriage on landing, although without injury to herself. Her courage and determination captured the imagination of the British public, and she was rewarded with a CBE from King George V plus a gift of £10,000 from the *Daily Mail*.

This startling achievement was followed by a series of other long-distance flights. In July 1931, she flew in de Havilland DH80A Puss Moth, letters G-AAZV (named 'Jason II') across Siberia to Tokyo. After arriving in the record time of ten days, she also broke the record for the return journey. In July of the following year, she married Jim Mollison, another long-distance pilot. In November and December of that year, she flew de Havilland DH80A Puss Moth letters G-ACAB (named 'Desert Cloud') to beat her husband's record for the solo flights to Cape Town and back.

In June 1933, Jim and Amy Mollison attempted a non-stop flight from England to New York in de Havilland DH84 Dragon I, letters G-ACCV, which they named 'Seafarer'. They ran out of fuel about sixty miles from their destination and crash-landed, both being injured. In October 1934, the couple made a record flight to Karachi in de Havilland Comet Racer letters G-ACSP, which they named 'Black Magic'. Amy made another solo flight to Cape Town and back in May 1936, in Percival Gull Six letters G-ADZO, beating the record for both flights.

Her marriage broke up in 1938 and she changed her name back to Amy Johnson. Although by this time she was covered with honours and was still considered a national heroine by the British public, Amy could not find

DH 80A Puss Moth letters G-AAZV, named 'Jason III', in which Amy Johnson broke the record from the UK across Siberia to Tokyo, as well as the return flight, in July 1931. *(Royal Air Force Museum AC77/36/7)*

Amy Johnson in May 1930 on arrival in Australia, after her solo flight from the UK in DH 80G Moth letters G-AAAH, named 'Jason'. *(Royal Air Force Museum AC77/36/4)*

Jim and Amy Mollison with DH Dragon I letters G-ACCV, named 'Seafarer'. In June 1933, they attempted to fly non-stop from England to New York in this machine but ran out of fuel and crash-landed sixty miles short of their objective. *(Aeroplane)*

Amy Johnson in her flying overalls before the unsuccessful attempt to fly non-stop from England to New York. *(Aeroplane)*

rewarding work in the male-dominated aircraft industry. She was at pains to present herself with the appearance of a sleek film star of the period and to modify her Yorkshire accent, but her private life was not happy. She suffered from bouts of depression, compounded by financial worries, and required medical attention. Nevertheless, she was an outgoing person, with a warm and generous nature, and other aviators liked and respected her.

At the outbreak of war, Amy was working for a firm in Portsmouth, flying aircraft on army co-operation and providing practice for anti-aircraft units with their range-finders and searchlights. On 20 May 1940, at a time when she had recorded 2,285 hours in her pilot's log book, she joined the Air Transport Auxiliary (ATA). This was a civilian organisation which resulted from a scheme introduced in May 1939 by Sir Francis Shelmerdine, the Minister for Civil Aviation at the Air Ministry. He recommended a reserve of private pilots, men and women, whose main duty would be to deliver aircraft from factories to RAF units. Thus those civilian pilots who for various reasons were unable to serve in the RAF could offer their experience in the national interest. The reserve was controlled by British Overseas Airways Corporation (BOAC), which in turn was formed from the amalgamation of the pre-war Imperial Airways and British Airways. Gerard d'Erlanger, a private pilot who had been a director of British Airways, was placed in charge.

By 30 September 1939, about thirty male pilots had been gathered together. After checking out at the Central Flying School, they were sent to join RAF ferry pools at Filton in Gloucestershire and Hucknall in Nottinghamshire. However, the mixture of civilian and RAF pilots did not work out very well and in February 1940 an all-civilian ferry pool was formed at White Waltham in Berkshire. Meanwhile, eight women pilots had been recruited in January 1940 and were based at Hatfield in Hertfordshire, which was part of the RAF's Flying Training Command.

On 15 February 1940, this civilian organisation was given the name of the Air Transport Auxiliary. In May 1940, Churchill formed a Ministry of Aircraft Production under Lord Beaverbrook, who saw the need for an expansion of the ATA to deliver the increased number of aircraft coming through the factories. The ATA grew rapidly during the summer until there were about a hundred pilots, including thirty women. These civilian pilots performed their essential service throughout the war and indeed suffered some distressing casualties, mainly as a result of flying in poor weather conditions.

At first, the women pilots were restricted to ferrying Tiger Moths, but they were soon cleared to fly the larger trainers such as the single-engined Master and Harvard as well as the twin-engined Oxford and Anson. It has to be recorded

Date.	Aircraft.		Engines.		Journey.		Time of Departure.		Time of Arrival.		Time in Air.		Pilot. See Instructions (5) & (6) on flyleaf of this book.
	Type.	Markings.	Type.	H.P.	From.	To.	Hrs.	Mins.	Hrs.	Mins.	Hrs.	Mins.	
						Brought forward	...	...	...	...	2542	50	
29.11.40	Anson	N.9978	Cheetah 9	350(2)	White Waltham	Hatfield					0	20	Self. Ferry
"	DH.86	X.9442	Gipsy 6		Witney	Cosford					0	45	" per Pilot
"	Rapide	R.9546	Gipsy 2		Hatfield	White Waltham					0	20	" Ferry
4.12.40	Oxford	T.1001	Cheetah 10	350(2)	Portsmouth	White Waltham					00	30	"
5.12.40	"	T.1002	"	"	"	Little Rissington					00	50	"
"	"	T.1015	"	"	"	"					00	55	"
7.12.4	"	T.1001	"	"	White Waltham	"					00	30	"
"	Hornet	N.7088	Gipsy	600	Kidlington	Kidlington					00	20	"
						Carried forward	...	...	...	...	2546	25	

A page from Amy Johnson's Pilot's Log Book held at the Royal Air Force Museum at Hendon. It is interesting to see that on 29 November 1940 she flew a four-engined de Havilland DH 86 from Witney in Oxfordshire to Cosford in Shropshire. (*Royal Air Force Museum*)

The de Havilland DH 86B was a larger version of the well-known Dragon Rapide, powered by four DH Gipsy Six engines of 200 hp and with auxiliary fins on the tailplane. A handful were employed by the RAF for communications duties and training wireless operators. This example was fitted with a loop aerial for wireless operators. (*Aeroplane*)

that Amy Johnson failed her first flying test when she joined the ATA, despite her great experience. Perhaps her main quality was enormous determination rather than careful handling of the aircraft, each of which needed to be delivered in one piece to its designated RAF unit. However, she soon qualified and was employed initially on providing a 'taxi service' for other ATA pilots, flying them to their destination in an Anson. It was not until December 1940 that she moved on to ferry work. By the end of that month she had entered another 275 hours in her pilot's log book, including 30 hours on the twin-engined Airspeed Oxford. At this stage, the women pilots did not deliver RAF operational aircraft and were confined to trainers.

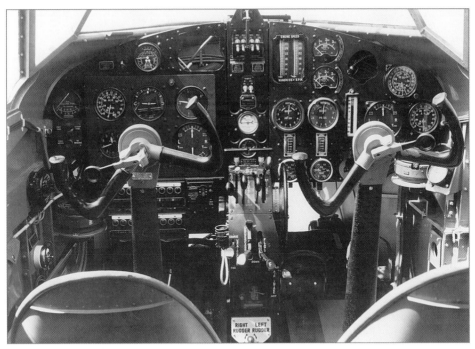

Dual control in an Oxford employed on advanced training for pilots. *(Aeroplane)*

On 3 January 1941 Amy was ordered by Pauline Gower, who commanded No. 5 Ferry Pilots Pool Women's Section at Hatfield, to ferry an Airspeed Oxford from that airfield to RAF Prestwick in Ayrshire. The weather closed in while en route and Amy landed at RAF Ternhill in Shropshire, spending the night in a hotel at Weston-under-Redcastle. When the weather cleared on the following day, she continued her journey and delivered the Oxford. After landing, she telephoned Pauline Gower on the tie-line to report her arrival and was told that she could either bring back another Oxford or take the night train from Glasgow to London if she felt too tired.

Amy jumped at the chance to return in another Oxford. The night train to London was always very overcrowded and often much delayed by air raids. She would probably have had to sit on her parachute in a crowded and unheated corridor and get no sleep in any event. Thus she took off in the Oxford and flew to RAF Squires Gate in Lancashire, arriving in the late afternoon of the same day. Here she stayed overnight with her sister Molly Jones and her husband Trevor, at their home in Blackpool.

The new Airspeed Oxford was due for delivery to RAF Kidlington in Oxfordshire, part of Flying Training Command, which had been the home of No. 15 Service Flying Training School (SFTS) since the previous October. Training was carried out primarily in single-engined North American Harvard

Is, but the number of twin-engined Oxfords was being steadily increased. The aircraft that Amy had been ordered to deliver was an Oxford II, serial V3540. It was a new machine, manufactured by de Havilland and delivered to No. 45 Maintenance Unit at Kinloss in Morayshire on 2 November 1940. This was primarily a holding unit, and its records show that no work was carried out to any Oxfords in that period. Thus the machine was not fitted with IFF (Identification of Friend or Foe) radar, nor did it carry the VHF transmitter and receiver TR9. Such equipment was usually fitted to Oxfords on arrival at training units.

This was the version without the dorsal turret, or indeed any armament at all. Its dimensions were similar to those of the Bristol Blenheim, a span of 53 ft 4 in, a length of 34 ft 6 in, and a height of 11 ft. Unfortunately the numbers of the Cheetah X engines were omitted from the official Aircraft Movement Card (AM Form 78).

At this stage in the war, training aircraft in Britain were painted in the conventional 'temperate land scheme' of dark green and dark earth on their upper surfaces and sides down to the bottom of the fuselage. The RAF roundels were red and blue on the upper wing surfaces, with red, white, blue and yellow on the sides of the fuselage. There were no unit codes, but the flash on the fin was the standard red, white and blue. However, they retained bright yellow on their undersurfaces. This was the distinctive colour which covered trainers entirely at the beginning of the war but the scheme had been modified for those within striking distance of the Luftwaffe. Serial numbers were painted in large black letters on the undersurfaces of the wings.

There were several witnesses to the circumstances of Amy's take-off from Squires Gate on 5 January 1941. After her death in the Thames, her father appointed the firm of solicitors with whom she had once worked in London, Messrs William Charles Crocker of Gracechurch Street, to obtain Probate of her Will in the High Court of Justice. In order to prove this will, it was necessary to establish her death without question in the eyes of the law. For this reason, signed statements were obtained from these witnesses. It was not easy to do this in wartime, since some of them were servicemen who had been posted to various parts of the world, and it was not until December 1943 that Amy's will could be proved. Today, all this information is available at the Department of Documents in the Royal Air Force Museum in Hendon. Other information, including some of the extra information I obtained, is available to researchers at the Public Record Office at Kew.

It is thus fairly simple to reconstruct the events which occurred before Amy took off on her last flight, from evidence supplied by the ground staff. Several

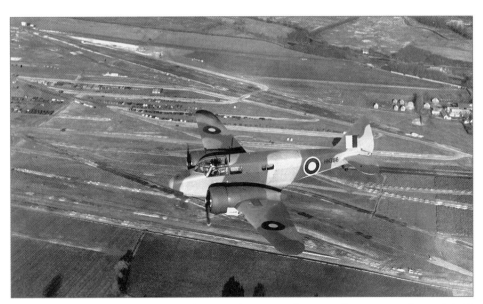

Airspeed Oxford II serial HN386, showing the camouflage on the upper surfaces. Bright yellow was retained on the undersurfaces. The Oxford II was powered by two Armstrong Siddeley Cheetah X engines of 375 hp. *(Author's collection)*

witnesses stated that Amy was wearing the dark blue uniform of the ATA, with trousers, and carrying a light-coloured bag. One of these witnesses was Frank Sutherland, a rigger in charge of the duty flight and employed by Brooklands Aviation Ltd. Squires Gate was used by civilian aviation companies as well as the RAF. Sutherland said that the fuel tanks of the Oxford, which other witnesses said were full when it left Prestwick, were topped up with about 32 gallons in the auxiliary tanks. He then said that Amy was advised by the duty pilot not to take off, since there was unfavourable weather ahead. Her response was to say that, once she had taken off, she would 'go over the top'.

Another witness was Harry Banks, a labourer and refueller employed by Brooklands Aviation. He said that Amy had a discussion with some RAF pilots about the weather before she entered the Oxford. He then got into the aircraft with her and they sat together for a while. The engines of the Oxford took as long as fifteen minutes to warm up in the cold weather. The oil temperature had to reach 25 degrees centigrade and the oil pressure 60lb per square inch. Amy gave him a cigarette and they both smoked and chatted. Smoking in RAF aircraft was forbidden but sometimes the rule was not observed. Banks noticed that Amy had a parachute strapped to her and that she had a light-coloured bag by her side. He got out only when she was ready to taxi out for take-off.

The various members of the ground staff gave their recollections of the time of take-off as between 1100 and 1149 hours. The most precise was an RAF aircraftman, Sidney J. Franklin, who was the airman of the watch. He said that a signal was sent to RAF Kidlington and that the signal log book recorded the time as 1149 hours. However, there was also a statement issued by the Ministry of Aircraft Production, which had overall control of the ATA. This gave the time as 1045 hours.

This apparent contradiction in times is one which I often encounter in my researches. It can be explained by the methods of recording times. During the war, local times in the UK were one hour in advance of the times we have today. British Double Summer Time (BDST) was in force in the summer months but British Summer Time (BST) – often called British Single Time – was in force for the remainder of the year. In 1941, BDST changed to BST at 02.00 hours on 10 August, so that Amy took off at 11.45 hours local time and the signal was sent four minutes later. The time of 10.45 hours for take-off must have been GMT, which was the method normally used in official service communications. It was known as 'Z time' or 'Zulu time', and was often used in instructions sent to RAF stations.

It is also possible to establish with considerable accuracy the state of the weather on 5 January 1941. I did this by a visit to the National Meteorological Archive at Bracknell in Berkshire, a method seldom employed by other researchers. Here, a person with some knowledge of meteorology and the synoptic charts used at the time may study not only the weather forecast for each day but, even more important, the *actual* weather conditions recorded at intervals throughout those days at 45 stations throughout the UK.

These records show that an anticyclone was centred over the north of England, with another anticyclone over southern Scandinavia. Visibility in the general area of Squires Gate was reported as two kilometres, or 2,187 yards. There was 2/10th cloud at 5,700 feet. The Operations Record Book of Squires Gate at the Public Record Office recorded visibility as very poor, but there was no cloud. It seems that Amy was entitled to take off in these conditions, for the minima decreed by the ATA were 800 feet cloud base and 2,000 yards visibility, although events were to demonstrate that Amy was unwise not to have heeded the advice of the duty pilot about the bad weather ahead.

Over the Midlands and south-east England, the high pressure system gave cloudy and dull conditions, with a wind on the surface of about 15 mph from the north-east. A thin layer of stratus cloud covered the entire area, invariably 10/10th (or 8/8th by the modern method of recording). The base of this cloud varied from 800 to 2,000 feet. There was almost no cloud at all above this layer of stratus. The ground was frozen hard and some areas were covered with snow. Visibility on the ground varied from fair to poor in occasional snow showers.

Such wintry conditions must be familiar to many flyers, an unbroken layer of low cloud with the sun shining on its upper surface, giving a meteorological 'inversion', with warmer air above a colder layer.

The temperature conditions within the cloud were such that icing conditions would have been experienced by aircraft flying through it. The records verify that this did happen. Balloons in the London area had to be hauled down and wiped. An ATA pilot who took off from Hatfield, Philippa B. Bennett, testified that when flying an Oxford to Scotland, ice crystals formed rapidly on the windscreen. She was just below the cloud base at the time but there was no sign of precipitation. She decided to return to Hatfield since, apart from her vision becoming obstructed, there was a danger of ice forming on the wings. The Oxford was fitted with carburettor heaters but not with wing de-icers. It would have been dangerous and unwise to have continued the journey.

The route that ATA pilots followed from RAF Squires Gate to RAF Kidlington was not a straight line, for it was necessary to avoid the prohibited areas of Liverpool, Crewe and the conurbation of towns to the west of Birmingham, especially those which were flying balloons. Thus there was a corridor of about four miles wide from Blackpool to the Mersey, between the balloon barrages of Liverpool and Widnes. From here, most pilots headed on a southerly track, keeping to the west of Kidderminster and hoping to pick up the landmark of the Severn. They skirted the radio masts of Droitwich, and then a turn to port gave the final leg to Kidlington. The total distance was about 130 miles, just over an hour's flying time in an Oxford.

It is probable that Amy intended to fly such a route, but the records show that she must have begun to fly over the low stratus cloud soon after leaving the Mersey. On arrival over the vicinity of Kidlington, it would have been very dangerous to let down through the low cloud, without an accurate knowledge of her position, for there were pylons and masts nearby as well as high ground. There was no R/T in the Oxford, nor were there direction facilities such as the Lorenz blind-approach system. She was alone in the aircraft and had to make up her own mind as to what to do in this predicament.

We cannot know positively why Amy decided to continue her flight instead of returning to Squires Gate, where the weather conditions were more favourable, but it is possible to make an informed guess. On 19 May 1987, I attended a ceremony at which a blue plaque was unveiled by English Heritage at Vernon Court in Hendon, where Amy lived in the early 1930s. At a gathering in the Royal Aircraft Museum afterwards, I was able to discuss this matter with several ex-ATA pilots. Most believed that Amy thought her reputation was such that she was *expected* to get through, even though other pilots might have turned back. ATA pilots could be disciplined for risking their lives and endangering their aircraft. On the following day, a party was to be held at Hatfield to celebrate the first anniversary of the Women's Ferry Pilots' Pool. This was precisely the occasion which Amy would have been determined to attend. She would have felt humiliated if she had been unable to be present.

When I asked the ex-ATA pilots what action they would have taken in similar circumstances on 5 January 1941, they were unanimous in saying that they would have turned back to Squires Gate. I have also put the same question to several ex-RAF pilots and navigators. Their replies were the same, with the proviso that if it had been essential to land at Kidlington, they would have flown over the lower and flatter land of East Anglia, or even over the coast, and then come down until land became visible. They would have kept under the cloud in an attempt to return to Kidlington. As an RAF navigator in 1941, I would certainly have done the same. My action would have been to head out over the sea before coming down through cloud, then pick up a position on the coastline before heading for the nearest airfield. But ATA pilots were under orders not to fly out of sight of the coast.

It is evident that Amy decided to head east for her main base of Hatfield and hoped to find a break in the clouds, either there or over the flat country of East Anglia. Of course, while above the clouds her aircraft could not be tracked by the network of posts of the Royal Observer Corps. Britain's network of RDF (or radar) stations did not operate inland but was directed to enemy aircraft approaching from over the sea. Map-reading and instinct were Amy's only guides, together with her P4 magnetic compass and the gyro compass in her instrument panel. Her words had been that she could 'feel her way' to Kidlington, but regrettably this optimisim had been unfounded.

The speculation that followed Amy's death has been fuelled by the genuine belief of several seamen who witnessed her last moments that they saw two people in the water. Indeed, after this tragedy ATA headquarters at White Waltham in Berkshire caused a signal to every RAF aerodrome, asking if Amy had landed to pick up a passenger. The answers were entirely in the negative.

Of course, it may be surmised that Amy might have disobeyed standing orders and landed in a field somewhere to pick up a passenger. But even if she had managed somehow to get down through the 10/10th cloud, she would have needed to find the field where the passenger was waiting. This would have needed to have had a length of at least 600 yards in order to take off again – in other words a small airfield. Short take-offs and landings were possible in the Oxford, but only after careful instruction at a flying training school, usually with a co-pilot to operate the flap lever. But Amy had not practised this advanced and somewhat dangerous procedure. Despite her long experience, she was not a proficient pilot in such techniques. Above all, it is generally agreed by her fellow pilots that, whatever her faults, Amy was intensely loyal and patriotic. She would never have disobeyed orders in this way. It is thus extremely difficult to see how, after Amy had taken off alone from Squires Gate, a passenger could have materialised in the aircraft.

Associated with the 'passenger theory', it has been surmised that Amy was engaged on some sort of clandestine mission to Occupied Europe, in collaboration with the Special Operations Executive. I can find no evidence in official records to support this contention. When special flights were made to Europe, somewhat later in the war, the aircraft used were black Lysanders flown only at night. These aircraft could land on a strip 150 yards in length, guided by agents using torches. While Amy was never short of courage, it is stretching the bounds of credulity too far to suggest that she disobeyed orders and flew during daylight in an unarmed trainer with bright yellow undersurfaces to land on an airstrip in enemy territory. Nor could the Oxford be used for parachuting agents. The only available exit for such a purpose was the door on the port side, aft of the mainspar, and this needed to be jettisoned to make the jump. It would not have been feasible to fly back with a missing door. Moreover, had the Oxford been used for a special flight over Europe, the point of take-off would have been somewhere near the south-east coast of England, not Lancashire.

Another proposition put forward by Amy's ex-husband, Jim Mollison, was that she had been shot down by an enemy aircraft. However, there is nothing in the German records to support this contention. Luftflotte 2, with headquarters in Brussels, was the German air fleet which operated over the Thames Estuary and the south-east of England. Luftflotte 3, with headquarters at St Cloud in Paris, was the air fleet which covered the south-west of England. It is true, as we shall see later, that both these air fleets despatched small numbers of bombers and reconnaissance aircraft over Britain on that day, but I have been able to establish from the Bundesarchiv (the German equivalent of the Public Record Office) that there were no combat reports, nor were any German aircraft lost.

All the available evidence points to the fact that Amy was simply trying to deliver her aircraft to Kidlington, as ordered, but ran into very bad weather. She was unwise not to have turned back, but it would be a very unusual pilot who could say that he or she never made an error of judgement in those dark days when Britain was fighting alone and courage was the main quality which enabled the country to survive. It is probable that Amy attempted to come down through the stratus cloud, maybe several times over flat ground, but encountered the windscreen icing which beset her friend Philippa Bennett, possibly accompanied by wing icing. She would have been too low to bale out when within the cloud. The logical course of action would have been to climb and hope to find a gap in the clouds before her fuel ran out. But there was something else which might have induced her to abandon the Oxford above 10/10th cloud over a particular position over the Thames Estuary.

At 1330 hours on 27 December 1940, nine days before Amy Johnson died, Squadron Leader Robert A. Barton DFC was flying a Hurricane I of No. 249 Squadron from North Weald in Essex. He was the commanding officer of the squadron and his task on this day was to lead a section of three Hurricanes over the Thames Estuary to protect Convoy CW20 on its way to Dover.

The weather conditions on this day were not dissimilar to those on the day when Amy died, although less severe. An area of high pressure was centred over Eire, giving low stratus over much of south-east England, although the ground temperatures were above freezing. This stratus was recorded as 9/10th over the Thames Estuary, and the pilots could not see the convoy they were supposed to escort. But they saw something else which interested them. A line of balloons was flying well above the low clouds, visible from ten miles away. They reported these during debriefing on their return.

It is probable that few pilots in those days realised that RAF crews handled the balloons in vessels that formed part of the coastal convoys, apart from the fighter pilots who were ordered to protect them. No. 11 Group of Fighter Command, to which No. 249 Squadron at North Weald belonged, made the perfectly reasonable assumption that those reported by the pilots were being flown from the convoy. It was thought ridiculous that they should be visible above cloud, advertising the presence of a convoy to enemy bombers. The purpose of balloons over both land and sea was to force these bombers higher, and spoil their aim. This was especially true of Junkers Ju87 dive-bombers, which had harried British coastal convoys since the fall of France and sunk a number of vessels. But, as it happened, No. 11 Group was wrong in that assumption.

The RAF's Balloon Command came under the authority of Fighter Command, and a letter of fairly mild reproof was sent from the latter to the former. In turn, the headquarters of Balloon Command sent a letter dated 2 January 1941 to the headquarters of its No. 30 (Balloon) Group, which was responsible for the activities of the balloon crews in the area in question. Again, the tone of the letter was only mildly reproachful, for it was realised that the crews could not raise and lower their balloons like yo-yos when the cloud base changed frequently. However, the letter asked No. 30 Group to ensure that balloons were flown below cloud so far as possible. Surprisingly, the reply sent from No. 30 Group, dated 7 January (two days after Amy's death), cleared the balloon crews of any charge of negligence. Something very unusual had happened over the Thames Estuary, and this requires a short explanation of the arrangement of the balloon defences around London.

When these defences were planned before the war, it was recognised that estuaries leading to large ports provided avenues through which enemy bombers could fly at low level to drop their loads accurately on targets. Something had to be done to close these gaps in the defences and arrangements were made to fly standard balloons, known as 'low zone' balloons, from barges moored across estuaries. In the Thames Estuary, thirty-two barges were moored between 00°43' East and 00°54' East, a band of sea seven miles wide between Southend-on-Sea on the north bank and Sheerness on the south. However, it was soon found that these barges could not weather the rough seas at the far entrance to the estuary, and the plan was modified in December 1939. East of a line running south from Shoeburyness on the north bank, the barges were replaced by drifters, small fishing vessels fitted with engines. These were moored at twelve sites across the estuary, on a line which stretched over the water for about five miles. Balloon-carrying barges were retained further towards London, where the waters were calmer.

A barge in the Thames Estuary, with its standard 'low zone' balloons close-hauled by the RAF crew. The RAF men and their balloon were part of No. 952 (Thames Barrage) Squadron. *(Bruce Robertson collection)*

A 'very low altitude' balloon, known in the RAF as the Mark VI and in the Royal Navy as the 'kite' balloon. It is being flown from an Admiralty drifter, the former Belgian *Richard Blonde* of 92 tons. This small balloon had a gas capacity of 1,240 cubic feet and was flown from a slender cable, up to 2,000 feet. Such balloons were flown from the smaller escort vessels in convoys and were also employed to prevent enemy aircraft from minelaying in narrow estuaries. The convoy over which Amy Johnson baled out was flying four of these balloons. *(The late Flight Lieutenant A.M. Puckle)*

The arrangement in these drifters was a truly British compromise. Each was manned by three or four RAF men to operate the balloon and its winch, but the drifter itself was manned by a civilian crew. The captain of each vessel was a civilian, who even had the authority to order the RAF men to cut the balloon adrift if he considered it necessary. The drifters were too small to bed down the balloons, but these could be close-hauled by the winches.

Thus, groups of RAF men were working on barges and drifters in the Thames Estuary, each man usually staying on board for about ten days before being relieved. The vessels were equipped with radio telephones and were visited regularly by supply boats. They formed part of No. 952 (Thames Barrage) Squadron of the RAF.

Of course, the Thames Estuary was visited regularly by the Germans. In the late summer of 1940, the introduction of acoustic mines combined with delay devices in magnetic mines created problems for the British when sweeping these intricate waters. At 1010 hours on 17 December 1940, one of these German mines exploded underneath the balloon drifter *Carry On* of 92 tons. She disintegrated and all the civilian crew and the RAF men on board were killed. Other mines were suspected and about an hour later it was decided to evacuate the six other drifters, partly because they included non-service personnel. There was no time to haul down the balloons and bring them to shore. In any case, these provided some defence against low-flying German aircraft, and they were left flying from the abandoned drifters.

These were the balloons which the Hurricane pilots had seen above the clouds on 27 December 1940, No. 30 Group explained to Balloon Command. On 3 January 1941, one of the abandoned drifters, *Newspray*, foundered in the night.

The 'Hunt' class escort destroyer HMS *Fernie* of 1,000 tons standard displacement, which was in the middle of the convoy when Amy Johnson baled out over the Thames Estuary on 5 January 1941. She was built by John Brown and launched on 9 January 1940. Her armament consisted of four 4 inch guns and four two-pounder guns, plus several 20 mm anti-aircraft guns. *(Maritime Photo Library)*

Five balloons were still flying from the drifters when Amy Johnson baled out near them on 5 January 1940, at a time when the other balloons in the defences of London had been hauled down below the clouds, for the base was only 800 feet in light snow showers.

These balloons must have been clearly visible above the cloud layer, acting as a marker above which she was flying, in the belief that she was over land and in the hope that a gap in the clouds would appear. According to No. 30 Group, the balloons were at 'about 2,000 feet', but the Hurricane pilots were in a better position to know and they saw them above that height. They were still in position when Balloon Command wrote to Fighter Command on 10 January 1940, and its explanation was accepted.

There were other balloons flying near the position where Amy drowned although some had been hauled down below the clouds. At 1230 hours GMT on 4 January 1941, the day before Amy's fateful flight, Convoy CE21 left Southampton bound for the Thames Estuary. This coastal convoy consisted of seventeen merchant vessels escorted by the Hunt class destroyers HMS *Fernie* and HMS *Berkeley*, both of 907 tons displacement, plus a French submarine chaser, two anti-aircraft trawlers, five balloon barrage vessels, four minesweepers and four motor launches. Each of the five balloon barrage vessels flew the smaller 'very low altitude' balloon. Every escort vessel carried anti-aircraft

The standard 'low zone' balloons flown by the vessels of the Mobile Balloon Barrage Flotilla. They were handled by RAF crews and were identical with those flown from barges and some drifters in estuaries, except that they were sometimes camouflaged on top with a checked pattern. The normal operating height was about 2,000 feet. The convoy over which Amy Johnson baled out flew five of these balloons. *(The late Flight Lieutenant A.M. Puckle)*

armament. Coastal convoys remained an essential part of the British economy, for neither the road system nor the railways could cope with the huge amount of traffic, especially in wartime.

The logs of the escort vessels in Convoy CE21 have not survived. However, the Public Record Office at Kew has a copy of the log kept by an officer in charge of the RAF crews in the nine balloon-carrying vessels, which gives details of times and positions on the convoy as well as the varying heights of the balloons as they were raised and lowered. This officer was Pilot Officer Anthony M. Puckle, and I was lucky enough to trace him when first researching this matter on behalf of *Aeroplane Monthly*.

Anthony Puckle was an experienced officer who had been an insurance broker at Lloyd's before the war. He had also gained his pilot's A Licence in 1938 at Redhill in Surrey and had joined the Auxiliary Air Force in the hope of serving as aircrew in some capacity if war broke out. But he was thirty years old and the RAF did not think anyone of this age was suitable for training. Instead, he was commissioned as a balloon officer and posted to No. 952 (Thames Barrage) Squadron at Sheerness.

Tony Puckle had sailed on the maiden voyage of the new Mobile Balloon Barrage, as it was named, on 4 August 1940. This had been formed soon after the fall of France from a motley collection of French and Belgian vessels which had managed to escape to England. It was evident that Britain's lifeline along the south coast had suddenly become very vulnerable to attacks from the Luftwaffe, and indeed this phase of the war became the prelude to the Battle of Britain. The RAF crews in these vessels formed 'Q' Flight of No. 952 (Thames Barrage) Squadron. At first, the balloons were flown at a height of 3,500 feet, but the German fighters simply shot them down while out of range of defensive light anti-aircraft fire. This was one of the reasons why the Junkers Ju87 Stuka dive-bombers were able to sink a number of vessels. The operating height was then brought down to 2,000 feet, with the heavier anti-aircraft guns set to explode 500 feet above, while the light anti-aircraft guns were within range of the enemy fighters. With greater experience among the ships' crews and more protection from Fighter Command, the convoys suffered fewer losses.

The Royal Navy commander of the Mobile Balloon Barrage Flotilla was Commander Garth H.F. Owles DSC, who was affectionately known as 'the Owl'. He normally sailed in the balloon barrage vessel HMS *Astral* but on 4 January 1941 sailed in HMS *Pingouin*, a tug of the French Navy which had been converted to a minesweeper. His place was at the head of the convoy. On this day, Tony Puckle sailed in HMS *Haslemere*, 756 tons. This was the balloon barrage vessel from which the crew tried to rescue Amy Johnson on the following day. *Haslemere* was one of five cross-Channel steamers which had been acquired in late 1940 to augment the Balloon Barrage Flotilla.

The captain of HMS *Haslemere* was Lieutenant-Commander Walter E. Fletcher RN. Aged thirty-four, his career had included a rather unusual episode, for in 1934 he had been seconded from the Royal Navy to serve as a navigator in a polar expedition led by J.M. Wordie of the Scott Polar Institute, across Baffin Land in northern Canada. He had a reputation for bravery. After he joined the Balloon Barrage Flotilla in September 1940, his vessel had come under heavy gunfire from the German emplacements at Cap Gris Nez. His sub-lieutenant had been killed beside him on the bridge and his first lieutenant wounded, but he had carried on coolly. Like Amy Johnson, he was a Fellow of the Royal Geographical Society, and both were to die in the same circumstances on the following day.

The nine balloon-carrying vessels formed a box round the merchant ships, with HMS *Pingouin* leading. HMS *Haslemere* sailed about halfway along the length of the convoy. At 1420 hours the convoy passed Portsmouth Gate, with the balloons flying at 2,000 feet. These were brought down to

Dover was attacked in the early morning of 29 July 1940 by Ju87 Stukas. Four of the dive bombers were brought down by anti-aircraft fire and RAF fighters. (*Author's collection*)

Lieutenant-Commander Walter E. Fletcher RN (left), talking to Lieutenant McKinlay RNR and Lieutenant Addis RNR on the bridge of the balloon-carrying vessel HMS *Haslemere*. Soon after this photograph was taken, he lost his life in a heroic but vain attempt to save Amy Johnson. *(The late Flight Lieutenant A.M. Puckle)*

200 feet during the night. Soon after passing Dover on the following day, 5 January, the balloons were raised to the cloud base, which in that area was about 1,800 feet.

When the convoy was passing through the channels of the Thames Estuary, several seamen saw a parachute come down through the clouds, followed by an aircraft which they thought was a Blenheim. Some seamen saw another object fall, which they thought might have been another person. The engines of the aircraft made no noise, but the machine circled the parachutist three times and then hit the water, which was described as rough, and then began to break up. Such manoeuvres are characteristic of a pilotless aircraft, and several pilots who have been forced to bale out have described similar circumstances to me. It seemed that a malignant fate in the form of the aircraft they had just left was trying to finish them off.

It is probable that Amy pointed the Oxford out to sea, throttled back and switched off the engines. The propellers were fixed pitch and could not be feathered. The normal procedure was to trim the aircraft in a slightly nose-down attitude, to prevent a stall. Then she must have moved back to the emergency exit, which was the small entry door in the port side of the fuselage aft of the wing. There was also an exit hatch in the cabin roof, but there was no point in using it in this emergency. The side door had to be jettisoned before jumping, and Amy either threw out two bags or left them in the entrance to fall away.

HMS *Haslemere* of 956 grt, from which the crew tried to rescue Amy Johnson when she baled out into the Thames Estuary in the afternoon of 5 January 1941. Built in 1925 by W.H. Henderson of Glasgow, she was employed by Southern Railways as a cross-Channel steamer until 22 October 1940, when she was taken over by the Royal Navy as a balloon-carrying escort vessel for coastal convoys. A gun platform can be seen on the bows in this wartime photograph. *(Maritime Photo Library)*

Amy's Last Flight
by Mark Postlethwaite GAvA

Amy Johnson prepares to bale out over the convoy's balloons flying above 10/10th cloud, after jettisoning the escape hatch of her Airspeed Oxford.

The absence of the door would have upset the trim of the Oxford and put it into a gentle spiral. The additional object which some seamen saw was probably either the door or one of these bags.

The time that this happened differs in various reports, some of which appear to depend on memory. According to the commander of HMS *Fernie*, it was 'about 1500 hours'. HMS *Haslemere* reported it as 15.30 hours. The most precise was the senior officer of the Motor Launch Flotilla, who recorded it as 1537 hours. However, the point to remember is that the Royal Navy kept its logs in GMT, as did navigators in the RAF when using air almanacs. Amy took off from Squires Gate at 1145 hours BST (1045 hours GMT), according to the most reliable information. She was thus in the air for over 4½ hours, and the maximum endurance of the Oxford was 4¾ hours. The Ministry of Aircraft Production stated soon afterwards: 'The machine carried fuel for only 4½ hours flight, the exact time which elapsed between the take-off and the crash.'

Amy is unlikely to have seen the convoy, since she was above 10/10th cloud at the time, but she may have seen some of its balloons. According to Tony Puckle's log, these were flown at 1,800 feet until the convoy entered the Medway Gate, a line leading south from Southend Pier. He said that it was the normal operating procedure at this stage in convoy warfare to bring them down below cloud unless there were enemy aircraft in the vicinity. As it happened, there were German bombers near the convoy and they were about to attack, some minutes after the Oxford hit the sea. Even if an order to bring down the balloons below the cloud base had been given, it would have taken some time to implement. The normal method of communication from ship to ship was by Aldis lamp, instructions being initiated from the commander of the leading balloon barrage vessel, accompanied by the message 'pass on' to the nearest vessel. The whole procedure took about fifteen minutes to travel down the length of the convoy.

In the documents preserved in the Royal Air Force Museum, there is a note in the handwriting of the investigating solicitor, William Crocker. It reads: 'Skipper Williamson says *Haslemere* had a balloon up at the time and is an Ack Ack ship and in charge of the convoy. Amy probably saw the balloons and thought she was over land and baled out. Snowing at the time.'

In fact, the overall command was in HMS *Pingouin*, under Commander Garth Owles, who was sailing in that vessel. Skipper Thomas Wilkinson was in command of the Admiralty drifter HMS *Young Jacob*, 99 tons, which sailed with the convoy as one of the four minesweepers.

The position of the crash of the Oxford was given by the Admiralty as 051°33'20" North 001°12'48" East. This was in Tizard Bank, near Knock John Buoy, with Black Deep to the north-east. To the south-west was Knob Channel, through which the convoy was sailing. The parachute splashed into the water behind the stern of HMS *Haslemere*, which immediately put on full speed and tried to turn back to give assistance. A turn to port was attempted at first but there was insufficient water in the narrow channel and she altered course to starboard. Today, the water in Tizard Bank varies from five to twenty feet. Depths can change in the Thames Estuary and there must have been shallow water at the time, for HMS *Haslemere* went aground. Her engines were put into slow astern.

Witnesses on the vessel said they saw two survivors, one quite clearly abreast the after hold, while the other was about forty yards away in the heavy sea. Tony Puckle also saw the more distant object, which he thought was a body, but he said to me: 'Of course, we were *looking* for survivors and in those circumstances we *assumed* it was a body.'*

The nearer object drifted towards the reversing vessel and to the surprise of the seamen was seen to be a 'fresh-faced women wearing a flying helmet'. She also appeared to be wearing a life jacket. The seamen heard her call out, 'Hurry, please hurry!' As the vessel moved closer to her, ropes were thrown over the side from the after deck. Two of these splashed alongside her, but she made no attempt to grasp them. About ten minutes had elapsed since Amy had landed in the bitterly cold water and she was probably numbed and shocked. The life jacket she appeared to be wearing must have been her parachute harness. It is evident that Amy did not follow the correct procedure when baling out over the sea, which was to turn and punch the release clip on the harness immediately before her feet entered the water. Weighed down with this harness while the silk parachute was dragging her in the strong incoming tide, she was being swept away rapidly from those attempting to rescue her.

Seaman Raymond A.C. Dean had mounted the bulwark aft of HMS *Haslemere* and got over the side to lie in the rubbing strake which acted as a fender. He steadied himself with one arm through the fairlead, an opening for a cable. When he saw that the woman was incapable of helping herself, he began to take off some of his clothes preparatory to diving to her rescue. But Lieutenant-Commander Fletcher came aft and ordered him to get back on board. At this point, Amy disappeared under the stern, which was heaving up and down, and was not seen again.

* When a version of this account was first published in *Aeroplane Monthly*, the editor received a very interesting letter from one of the readers, Philip N. Owen, who had spent much of his wartime RAF service in units equipped with Oxfords. On one occasion, he saw a door fall off an Oxford. It turned over and over in the air, and could easily have been mistaken for a body. He also said that the hollow door would have floated in the water, and might have been mistaken for a person's head and shoulders.

Airspeed Oxford V serial EB490, showing the bright yellow undersurfaces with large black lettering. The Mark V was powered by two Pratt & Witney Wasp-Junior R-985-AN6 engines of 450 hp and employed mainly on navigation training. *(Aeroplane)*

An early publicity photograph of a pilot in the Women's Section of the Air Transport Auxiliary (ATA), kitted out with a Sidcot flying suit and a seat parachute. *(Bruce Robertson collection)*

Then Walter Fletcher stripped off his duffel coat, boots and uniform, and dived over the side. He swam towards the more distant object which the men thought was another survivor, and reached it. While he was swimming, the ship's lifeboat was launched and the oarsmen tried to reach their captain in the heavy seas. 'For God's sake, lad, tell them to pull!' Fletcher shouted to Seaman Vivian Gray in the lifeboat. But the men had not been trained to row in unison and the wind and the tide were against them. The rudder seemed useless and the steering oar broke. Try as they might, they could not keep the bows in the correct direction, although they were only a few yards away from Fletcher.

As this point, the motor launch HMS *ML113* came to the rescue. This motor launch was standing away in the shallow water, but the men threw a Carley float over the side. Three men clambered down into it and began to paddle towards Fletcher. Then something significant happened. Fletcher abandoned whatever he was holding and began to swim towards the Carley float. Readers must ask themselves whether a man who was capable of such bravery would have abandoned a survivor, or whether he was holding something else. Lieutenant George A. Wright of the Royal Marines, one of the men in the Carley float, stripped off his outer clothes and swam towards Fletcher, who was obviously in difficulties. He reached him, supported him back to the Carley float, and the men were soon back on board HMS *ML113*. Fletcher had been in the water for about ten minutes and was unconscious. A doctor was brought aboard from the destroyer HMS *Fernie*, but artificial respiration and other measures failed to revive Fletcher. He was still alive when the motor launch reached Sheerness and was rushed to the naval hospital HMS *Wildfire*, but it was stated later that he had died from immersion hypothermia.

The crew of HMS *ML113* did not know the identity of the man they had brought out of the sea. He was not wearing a uniform or even his identity discs, but they assumed he was a seaman from HMS *Haslemere*. Later in the day, signals were sent from the hospital, asking various Royal Navy and RAF units if anyone was missing. Eventually Walter Fletcher was identified by Lieutenant Henry P. O'Dea, the first officer of HMS *Haslemere*.

After Amy landed in the sea, the Luftwaffe attacked the convoy. The commanding officer of HMS *Fernie* stated in a report dated 6 January 1941 addressed to the Commander-in-Chief, The Nore (the Royal Navy's major base at Chatham in Kent) that the rear ship in the convoy was bombed by a Junkers Ju88 and that the destroyer HMS *Berkeley* had opened anti-aircraft fire. This was at 1600 hours GMT, about half an hour after Amy had come down.

The German records confirm this engagement. About 45 bombers and reconnaissance aircraft, but no fighters, were despatched by Luftflotte 2 and

Luftflotte 3 over Britain during daylight hours on 5 January 1941. Of these, nine from Luftflotte 3 were detailed to attack London, but three turned back owing to the bad weather. However, the cloud base was higher over the Low Countries and a few German aircraft were able to slip underneath it towards south-east England. The German records state: 'A convoy of sixty-two ships entering the Thames Estuary was attacked by various units, but with limited success.' This report exaggerated the number of ships and in fact achieved no success since no British ships were sunk or even damaged.

Immediately after the flurry of activity with the bombing, the destroyer HMS *Berkeley* put a whaler over the side to search the area where Amy baled out. The seamen did not find a survivor or a dead body but they recovered two bags floating in the water. One had the letters 'AJ' on the side while the other bore the name 'Amy Johnson'. The contents were later identified by Mrs Molly Jones as belonging to her sister Amy Johnson. Her pilot's log book was in one of the bags and is now housed in the Royal Air Force Museum. It is inconceivable that she would have carried this if she had been engaged on some clandestine operation over enemy territory.

Some hours after these bags were recovered, the drifter HMS *Young Jacob* recovered some aircraft wreckage about three miles away. Skipper Thomas Williamson took this to his base at Brightlingsea in Essex. It included a piece of bright yellow fabric with the letters '35', which was eventually handed to the solicitor William Crocker. In turn, it was shown to Pauline Gower of the ATA, who identified it as part of Amy's aircraft, Oxford serial V3540. On 8 January 1941, wreckage which appeared to be part of the fin of an Oxford was washed up on the mud flats off Shoeburyness.

During the daylight hours of 5 January 1941, Fighter Command's No. 11 Group, which covered the south-east of England, attempted to send up a number of Hurricanes and Spitfires, but the bad weather prevented any take-offs from Kenley, Biggin Hill, Martlesham Heath, Debden or Southend. Pauline Gower was told later that Amy's Oxford had been tracked by some of the coastal radar stations and was recognised to have been in trouble. This might well have been possible during the period it was over the Thames Estuary. The Oxford was not equipped with IFF (Identification of Friend or Foe), but since it did not arrive from enemy territory it was obviously a British aircraft flying to and fro.

Pauline Gower was also told that fighter pilots were ordered to look for the machine and try to guide it to safety. North Weald managed to put up two Hurricanes in the morning and two in the afternoon, all of them over the area of Clacton, but bad weather prevented contact of any description. Hornchurch put up two Spitfires in the morning and two more in the afternoon, over the

Thames Estuary, but these did not report anything. There is nothing in the terse squadron records to confirm that they were told to look for a stray British aircraft, although this may well have happened. Other than Amy's Oxford, no aircraft were lost by either the British or the Germans in this area, and neither side reported any sightings or combats.

One of the most ridiculous theories about the death of Amy Johnson appeared in several British national newspapers in February 1999, under such headlines as 'I shot down Amy Johnson's plane' and 'Friendly fire killed Amy Johnson'. This originated from a retired gardener who was serving as a gunner with the 58th (Kent) Heavy Anti-Aircraft Regiment on the day of her death. He was stationed at Iwade in Kent, on the Thames Estuary, and was ordered to fire when the aircraft 'failed to cite the colour of the day'. At this, 'sixteen rounds of shells were fired into the sky and the aircraft dived into the Thames Estuary'. The gunners 'thought it was an enemy plane until we saw the newspapers the next day and realised it was Amy Johnson'.

But if one examines the position of Iwade and that of the crash of Amy Johnson's Oxford, it is clear that they are over twenty miles apart. Not even heavy anti-aircraft guns had that range. Moreover, if one examines the war diary of the 58th (Kent) Heavy Anti-Aircraft Regiment, which is readily available to any reader at the Public Record Office, it states that the battery did not open fire until 1800 hours and that firing continued until midnight. Thus an hour and a half had elapsed from the time Amy came down and the time when this battery first opened fire. The war diary is signed by the commanding officer, Lieutenant-Colonel H.J. Hedley RA. Other official records state that the London defences fired 1,639 heavy artillery shells into the air against thirty-six German bombers during that night. None of these could possibly have hit Amy Johnson's Oxford, which had already broken up in the Thames.

Perhaps the most surprising aspect of this newspaper item is the credence which some journalists gave to the fantasy without bothering to carry out the most basic and elementary checks. But had they done so it would have spoilt the story, which might not have been to their liking.

Amy Johnson had often pointed out that her accidents always happened on Sundays, and she thought that this was the unlucky day of the week for her. The 5th of January 1941 was also a Sunday. Everyone who risks his or her life frequently can expect only a quota of good luck. Amy must have used up most of hers during the dangerous flights she undertook before the war. Several factors combined against her on the day of her death. The unbroken cloud gave extremely difficult conditions for flying in a training aircraft without wing de-icers or any special navigational equipment. The balloons provided a trap into

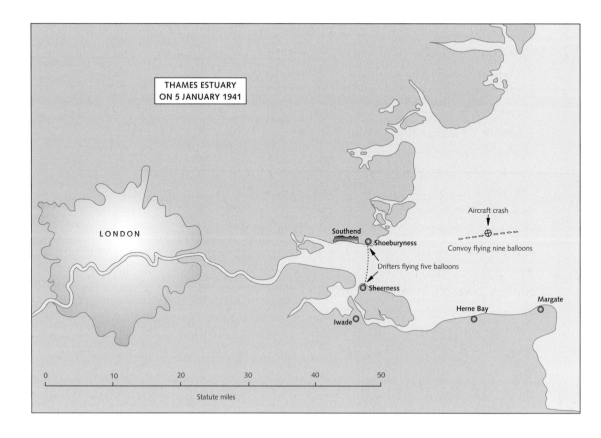

which she fell, probably in the belief that she was over land. This was a greater tragedy since land was only a few minutes flying time away. The final catastrophe, not only for Amy but for the gallant Walter Fletcher, was the fact that she came down into water which was so shallow that rescue by HMS *Haslemere* could not be effected. But her life and achievements must place her for ever as a heroine in the history of British aviation.

In January 2002 the above analysis was read by Master Engineer Phil Nobbs of the VC10 Training Flight, RAF Brize Norton, who is the special projects officer for the RAF Sub-Aqua Association. After careful checking of facts, members of this Association* decided to mount an expedition in an attempt to recover some parts of the Airspeed Oxford from the Thames Estuary.

It was recognised immediately that a whole aircraft could not be found, since the machine began to break up after hitting the water and some parts had been recovered from the sea or washed up on the shore. The most likely remains to be on the sea bed were two Cheetah X engines plus perhaps part of the

* See Chapter Three for details of the Association.

undercarriage. These could not have floated very far from the position of the crash but would have sunk quickly. Moreover, the position recorded by the Royal Navy may not have been precisely accurate, for navigational systems such as GPS, which gives locations within a few feet, were not available at the time.

After a considerable amount of discussion and preparation, a preliminary dive took place in July 2002. This was preceded by a visit to the Rolls-Royce Heritage Trust, for an examination of a Cheetah X engine on display, and correspondence with the Port of London Authority, since acceptance of the times and places of any dives had to be granted. The RAF diving team, all of whom volunteered in their off-duty periods, were experienced and highly proficient. They acquired a rigid inflatable boat (RIB) from the RAF Sub-Aqua Association at Brize Norton, a GPS and a magnetometer, and decided to operate from Herne Bay as the nearest convenient port to the position of the crash. They were gratified by the support and enthusiasm received from all concerned with their project.

The team knew that the currents were extremely strong in these waters, so that diving was possible only in short periods of slack water when the tide was

The Rigid Inflatable Boat (RIB) of the Royal Air Force Sub-Aqua Association at Herne Bay, together with a diving team. Left to right: Flight Sergeant Andy Weston; Flight Lieutenant Pete Hawkins; Chief Technician Steve Clark; Sergeant Patch Swindle. *(RAF Sub-Aqua Assn)*

Chief Technician Steve Clark of the RAF Sub-Aqua Association with a Cheetah X Armstrong Siddeley engine at the Rolls-Royce Heritage Trust. The team of divers examined this example before beginning their expedition. *(Rolls-Royce Heritage Trust)*

on the turn, and that the channel was in one of the busiest shipping lanes in the world. In the event, the swirling current in slack water proved so strong that each pair of divers had to descend on a weighted 'shot line' to arrive at the correct position. They knew that visibility would be very limited and in fact it proved to be no more than two feet at best and sometimes nil. They found that the bottom was like soft mud, so that the engines of the Oxford must have sunk and become covered with silt. It was disconcerting to be in a fragile boat while large sea-going vessels were bearing down on them, but the Port of London Authority had informed all shipping and some of these vessels signalled encouragement.

Despite all these difficulties, the team (which will vary in accordance with the personnel available at any one time) became determined to continue. The RAF convened a meeting at Brize Norton on 20 August 2002, attended by many concerned with the project, as well as journalists and TV teams. The inflatable boat was on display, together with an underwater metal detector which is now considered necessary for the hunt. Dives are continuing until November 2002 and if necessary will be resumed in April or May 2003. The RAF is making a determined attempt to find and raise the engines of this machine, as a tribute to Britain's foremost woman aviator.

CHAPTER THREE

Beauforts under Water

Until recent years, the operations carried out by Bristol Beauforts in the Second World War have been almost ignored by air historians. This is possibly because it was a 'strike aircraft' of Coastal Command, which has never captured the imagination of the general public so vividly as Fighter Command or Bomber Command. The Battle of Britain and the bombing of Germany tend to dominate histories of the air war, while operations against enemy surface vessels seem to be of less significance. Yet the activities of Coastal Command and the maritime squadrons abroad were arguably of equal importance to the Allied victory. The part played by Beauforts, both at home and abroad, was dramatic and certainly made a valuable contribution to the prosecution of the war.

Three Beaufort Is of No. 22 Squadron carrying torpedoes in 1941. The nearest aircraft is fitted with a blister gun under the nose. This was fired backwards by the navigator, with an arrangement of mirrors, as protection against a belly attack. *(Author's collection)*

A torpedo being wheeled to a Beaufort I, past the blister gun underneath the nose. *(Author's collection)*

The Bristol Beaufort was a twin-engined monoplane designed as 'the fastest torpedo bomber in the world'. The Mark I was powered by two Bristol Taurus VI engines of 1,130 hp. The maximum speed was 265 mph at 6,000 feet and the normal endurance was about six hours. It was crewed by a pilot, navigator, wireless operator and gunner, and could carry up to 2,000lb of bombs or a single torpedo. The armament of the early aircraft consisted of a single 0.303 inch Browning in the port wing and a single 0.303 inch Vickers K gun in the power-operated dorsal turret, although two more Vickers K guns could be mounted in beam positions and fired by the wireless operator and navigator.

Beauforts first entered squadron service in November 1939 with No. 22 Squadron at Thorney Island in Sussex. This squadron moved to North Coates in Lincolnshire in the following April. No. 42 Squadron at Thorney Island was the next to receive Beauforts, in April 1940, before moving to Wick in Caithness in the following June. Coastal Command squadrons changed their bases far more frequently than those of Bomber Command, and often sent detachments to other stations. No. 217 Squadron at St Eval in Cornwall received its first Beauforts in May 1940, but did not become fully operational with these new machines for several months. The last in the UK to receive Beauforts and employ them operationally was No. 86 Squadron, when based at North Coates in June 1941.

There was an initial shortage of pilots trained in torpedo work and insufficient torpedoes for the squadrons. The early operations carried out by the Beaufort squadrons consisted mainly of low-level bombing attacks on ships, minelaying outside enemy harbours and bombing attacks on dock installations. The first machines suffered from technical defects and in any event could not fly on one engine for a sustained period.

The Beaufort was a robust machine, but the nature of its work was without doubt the most hazardous in the RAF. Low-level operations were often carried out in daylight and then came under point-blank enemy fire. On 16 November 1942 the Air Member for Training, Air Marshal Sir A. Guy R. Garrod, reported that the chances of surviving a single tour in an RAF torpedo bomber squadron was no more than 17½ per cent, or merely 3 per cent in two tours. This could be compared with squadrons of the heavy and medium bombers, where the chances of survival were 44 per cent in one tour or 19½ per cent in two tours.

During the period I served in No. 217 Squadron, from January 1941 to March 1942, we lost thirty-six aircraft and crews, while our normal strength was probably no more than fifteen crews. Other squadrons suffered the same casualty rate, or even worse. At the end of the war, every Beaufort still in existence was scrapped. There seemed to be no storage space or finance to keep as museum pieces some of the RAF aircraft which had served their country so well, and air history is the poorer for this neglect.

The navigator's position in the nose of a Beaufort, with a 'course-setting' bombsight looking forward, instruments on the right, a chart table on the left and a blister gun underneath. *(Author's collection)*

On 3 September 1989, the 50th anniversary of the outbreak of Britain's war with Germany, Mrs Bente Mary Sväsand was walking in the mountains above Böröy fjord in her native Norway, together with a family friend. The fjord is in the administrative district of Bömlo, an inland area which can be reached only by ferry from the mainland. Dates relating to the Second World War are important to Europeans whose country was occupied by Germany, even to those who were not born at the time. The talk was of the war, when Bente's friend remarked:

'Did you know that the body of an English airman was found near the islands of Big and Little Flatöy?'

Bente was intrigued. She had been to school in England, for her mother was English, and had always been interested in the RAF. Indeed, she had tried to join the WRAF when she was younger, but her application had been turned down, for her father was Norwegian. That walk in the mountains set off a train of events which would occupy her spare time for the next two years, and the matter became almost an obsession with her.

It seemed to Bente Sväsand that a memorial should be erected to the RAF men who had died in the fjord, to commemorate the 50th anniversary, but first many details had to be established. Helped by a former schoolfriend in England,

Mrs Sandra 'Sandy' Sanders, Bente began the task. The two ladies discovered that the aircraft was a Bristol Beaufort Mark I of No. 42 Squadron, based at Leuchars in Fife, which had failed to return from a sortie on the night of 12/13 August 1941. Neither had ever heard of a Beaufort, but they learnt about my books and articles concerning the squadrons equipped with this machine, and also that there was a Beaufort Aircrews Association. A letter sent to my first publisher, William Kimber, was returned, for this company had been taken over a few years before and no longer existed at its former address. However, another letter sent to the aviation author Chaz Bowyer was forwarded to me. Bente, Sandy and I continued the research together and eventually met in the Royal Air Force Club in Piccadilly, London.

The night of 12/13 August 1941 was very busy for No. 42 Squadron. Nine Beauforts took off at about midnight, heading for the port of Haugesund in Norway, on 'Operation Bottle'. Three of the aircraft carried four 250lb bombs with eleven-second delays in tail fuses, to make low-level attacks against the dock installations as a diversion for the remaining six, which carried 'cucumber' magnetic sea mines of about 1,500lb to drop on the sea bed outside the harbour entrance.

There was a full moon and a south-westerly wind, but a depression gave overcast and showery conditions, so that visibility was moderate to poor. One aircraft carrying a mine blew up shortly after take-off and the four crew members were killed. This type of accident was not uncommon with these sensitive weapons, although the reasons were not fully understood. In my squadron, it was believed that the soluble capsule protecting the firing mechanism, designed to dissolve in sea water and arm the weapon while it was resting on the sea bottom, was sometimes affected by rain water so that it was set off by the metal of the aircraft. The remaining eight aircraft continued to Haugesund. Two of these could not locate their targets and returned to Leuchars. Three of the others dropped mines, while two bombed the docks, encountering concentrated light flak and spotting a Messerschmitt Bf109.

Beaufort serial AW200 letter R, which was carrying bombs, failed to return. In the early hours of that night, Norwegians living near the south-east tip of the island of Böröya heard this aircraft approaching in a northerly direction, from Haugesund and across Böröy fjord. An engine was coughing and a line of tracer was seen, probably from a flak ship. The machine was heard to ditch and then there were cries for help.

Some Norwegians were hesitant about rowing out, for there was a Quisling in the locality and the area was a centre for Norwegian Resistance. It was from this fjord that the famous 'Shetland bus' sometimes sailed. This was the name for the series of small fishing boats which took men and intelligence to Britain and then returned with men trained in clandestine operations plus their equipment. Penalties for those who helped Germany's enemies in August 1941 were already severe, but Sigurd Barane, who was returning from a fishing trip, rowed towards the position of the man calling for help. After about an hour he found the body of an airman floating in his Mae West lifejacket, near the islands of Big and Little Flatöy. This was one of the wireless operator/air gunners, Sergeant Edward Roy Harcourt, who seemed to have died in the water after striking his forehead against some part of the Beaufort.

Bente was told that the Norwegian also found a dinghy, a wheel, two fuel tanks, part of a wing, a seat covered with foam rubber, and the Mae Wests of the other three crew members with their names written on them. The bodies of these three crew members were not found. In a pocket of Harcourt's flying suit, Sigurd Barane found a pencilled note stating that the aircraft had engine trouble and that they were looking for somewhere to land. This note was collected by the Germans, and eventually the airman was buried in a cemetery in Bergen, with the usual military ceremony which both the British and the Germans accorded to their enemies.

Sergeant H.G. Norman Morison DFM (photographed as a trainee), the pilot of Beaufort AW200 of No. 42 Squadron who lost his life on 13 August 1941. *(Kenneth E.J. Morison)*

Sergeant Robert McNab, one of the two wireless operator/air gunners who lost their lives in Beaufort AW200 of No. 42 Squadron on 13 August 1941. *(Graham McNab)*

Harcourt was thirty years of age, unmarried and born in Bristol. He was the oldest in the crew, all of whom were sergeants. The pilot was Henry Gordon Norman Morison DFM, who had enlisted in the RAFVR immediately war was declared. He was unmarried, aged twenty-one, and his parents lived in Swansea. The navigator was Henry Gaunt Gibbon, aged twenty-eight, who had joined the RAFVR before the war as a 'weekend flier'; he came from Hanley in Staffordshire and was married, with two children. The other wireless operator/air gunner was Robert MacNab, unmarried and aged twenty-one, from Grangemouth in Stirlingshire. He was the only man in the regular RAF, which he had joined in March 1939. He had flown in Morison's crew twice before and replaced the normal gunner, Sergeant Tyler, on this sortie.

The question of the three Mae Wests taken from Böröy fjord is curious. In my Beaufort squadron, our crews wore these lifejackets on every operation, but I am assured by a former crew member that only the gunners in No. 42 Squadron wore their Mae Wests and parachute harness all the time, whereas some of the other crew members did not put them on unless there was an emergency. It has to be assumed that either Harcourt was in the turret on this occasion, or else he was the only one of the other three who was able to slip on his lifejacket before the Beaufort hit the water. By coincidence, Morison and Harcourt, together with Sergeants Cawthorne and Tyler, had survived a ditching on 24 May 1941, when their starboard engine cut during a daylight convoy escort. The four men had got into their dinghy and were picked up unharmed by a destroyer.

Morison was known in No. 42 Squadron as a dashing and adventurous pilot who flew the Beaufort

Sergeant H. Gaunt Gibbon (photographed as a leading aircraftman), the navigator who lost his life in Beaufort AW200 of No. 42 Squadron on 13 August 1941. *(Mrs Hilda E. Sherwin)*

The grave of Sergeant Edward Roy Harcourt, wireless operator/air gunner of No. 42 Squadron, at Möllendahl Cemetery in Bergen. *(Mrs Bente Mary Sväsand)*

like a fighter. He had received an immediate award of a DFM only a few days before his last flight, for he had carried out a remarkable sortie on 25 July 1941. On that occasion, his Beaufort arrived over the south-west coast of Norway at dawn, following a delayed take-off from Leuchars, and the crew found a ship off Egero. This was *Vestkyst I* of 370 tons, which they bombed and sank. The ship's crew took to the lifeboat. Morison then gunned Mandal lighthouse, which was believed to be a German observation post. Following this, he made three separate bombing runs over the nearby airfield. The crew then turned for home, but inevitably two Messerschmitt Bf109s from Mandal airfield caught up with the Beaufort and attacked.

MacNab was also in the turret on this sortie, and shouted a warning. The navigator was Sergeant C.W. 'Buster' Hayes, who eventually retired from the RAF as a Group Captain with an OBE. He had replaced Gibbon, who was in discomfort with toothache. Hayes went back and took up station on the starboard waist gun, while Harcourt manned the gun at the port entry hatch. Morison threw the aircraft around the sky, while the three gunners fired at the Messerschmitt Bf109s and shot one down. It was flown by *Leutnant* Minz of *Jagdgeschwader* 77, whose body was never recovered. Hayes then saw the German pilot of the other Messerschmitt salute before turning for home. The Beaufort men assumed that he had used up all his ammunition or fuel.

Bente and I combined in trying to locate relatives of the four Beaufort men who had lost their lives on 13 August 1941, using public records and advertisements. It proved a long and difficult process, but eventually they were traced. Harcourt's family was the most difficult for, unknown to us, his grandfather was an immigrant from Poland who had changed his name from Bette to Bennett, and then his father had assumed the name Harcourt-Bennett. However, some cousins answered an advertisement in the Royal Air Force Association's magazine *Air Mail* of July 1991.

Meanwhile, I had approached the vice-chairman of the RAF Sub-Aqua Association, Squadron Leader John Botham, who was in course of taking up a new appointment as Officer Commanding Operations Squadron at

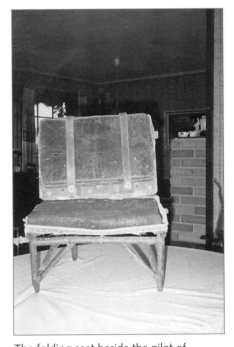

The folding seat beside the pilot of Beaufort serial AW200, which came to the surface after the crash in Böröy fjord. It is still covered in foam rubber.
(Mrs Bente Mary Sväsand)

The two friends who began the investigation into the crash of Beaufort serial AW200, photographed in Norway. Left to right: Mrs S. 'Sandy' Sanders; Mrs Bente Mary Sväsand. *(Mrs Bente Mary Sväsand)*

Chivenor. Although we were aware that the RAF Museum would acquire a Beaufort within the next few months, this machine was being rebuilt from parts manufactured in Australia, and at this time no Beaufort built in Britain existed anywhere in the world. Thus the location of a Beaufort in a Norwegian fjord seemed to us of historic importance. The RAF Sub-Aqua Association decided to mount an expedition.

Lest any readers should think that it is simple to arrange an underwater search in Norway, culminating in an unveiling ceremony of a memorial, I can assure them that the process requires the wisdom of Solomon combined with the patience of a saint. Bente worked miracles in Norway, writing hundreds of letters, lobbying the Council of the local Bömlo Kommune, flying to and from England, arranging the reception of relatives and guests, helping with the physical work of the memorial, and finding a suitable site and boat for the RAF team. These matters required about two years of unflagging effort, supported by encouragement from some local people and a grant of £2,500 from the Council for the memorial and the unveiling ceremony.

Similarly, John Botham had to overcome snag after snag for eighteen months. The RAF Sub-Aqua Association had been established for about twenty-three years and consisted of about 60 clubs with a total membership of around 600. It was sponsored by the RAF Sports Board, which encouraged 'adventurous training' and provided a yearly grant. Members had dived in distant parts of the world, such as the barrier reef off Belize. They were interested in old harbours, archaeology, underwater wrecks and the examination of marine behaviour. They operated under the wing of the British Sub-Aqua Club and observed its rules, being careful of the environment and shunning such sports as the spearing of fish. In June 1973, they had raised Halifax serial W1048 of No. 35 Squadron from Lake Hoklingen in Norway, before it was removed to the RAF Museum in Hendon.

However, the RAF Sub-Aqua Association had to rely on outside support for the loan of some equipment as well as for much of the funding of expeditions.

To hunt for Beaufort serial AW200, specialised equipment needed to be borrowed and diplomatic clearance obtained. There was also the possibility that the remains of the aircraft might be classed as a War Grave and thus should be left undisturbed. Much of John Botham's other work concerned the raising of finance, but support was received from several bodies, such as British Aerospace. The commanding officer of No. 42 Squadron at St Mawgan showed great interest and was kept informed of progress.

Before the sub-aqua team left, the Squadron Navigation Leader of No. 42 Squadron, Squadron Leader Ian Coleman, discussed with me the possibility of a flypast of a Nimrod from RAF St Mawgan to coincide with the unveiling ceremony. An official letter was then sent from the Bömlo Kommune inviting the squadron to participate. Authority for the flypast was granted by the RAF's No. 18 Group, to be incorporated in a scheduled training flight off Norway.

The municipality of Bömlo consists of a series of islands with about 10,000 inhabitants, inland from the west coast between Bergen and Stavanger. It is a beautiful, green and peaceful area which is visited only by knowledgeable Norwegians and tourists, for access to the mainland is solely by ferry. The journey by hydrofoil from Bergen lasts about two hours. The site chosen for the RAF memorial was on a cliff at the north of Böröy fjord, overlooking Big and Little Flatöy, near where Beaufort serial AW200 plunged into the water.

On 1 August 1991, an RAF sub-aqua team of seven men left Newcastle on Tyne on a ferry bound for Bergen. They were Squadron Leader John Botham from Chivenor, Warrant Officer Dave Whitehall from St Mawgan, Flight Sergeants Sandy Bange from Mount Batten and Ian Mackay from Hereford, Sergeant Bill Rowlands from Chivenor, and Corporals Trevor Frampton from Locking and Al Goodwin from Helston. They were accompanied for a few days by Joe Haskins of Dowty Maritime.

In addition to their diving gear the team brought with them a sidescan sonar loaned by Dowty Maritime and a Trisponder navigation system from Del Norte Technology. The RAF and the Royal Navy provided other equipment. The Norwegians had offered the use of a 28 foot fishing boat, the *Fjordbris*, as well as a camp site close to the search area. Only ten days had been allotted for the work in the fjord.

The men of the RAF Sub-Aqua Association did not succeed in their quest, but not for want of effort. Ten days is not long and things did not go well from the start. The Norwegians had withdrawn permission for the use of the sonar only two days before they arrived, since the area was considered militarily sensitive. However, after many phone calls and three lost days, permission was restored. The lost time was spent in rigging up their site and checking equipment. Bad

The RAF sub-aqua team carrying out a sonar search in Böröy fjord from the fishing boat *Fjordbris*, loaned by the Norwegians. *(Sergeant Bill Rowlands)*

RAF divers returning to the surface of Böröy fjord, passing some of the jellyfish found in these waters. *(Flight Sergeant Ian MacKay)*

weather dogged some of the remaining time, giving choppy waters in the fjord. But the major problem proved to be the nature of the bottom of the fjord, which consists of masses of rocks in deceptive shapes, interspersed with stretches of mud. Moreover, the depth of the bottom changed constantly as the boat progressed, requiring frequent adjustments to the sonar equipment.

We had calculated in advance the probable site of the crash, based on the northerly current in the fjord and the time interval before Harcourt's body was recovered. However, while the RAF men were working, Norwegian witnesses gave slightly different positions for the crash site, so alterations in the area of search were made. There was a period of hope when the sonar indicated the shape of an aircraft, but this proved to be a deceptive rock formation. The RAF men were unable to complete their work before it became necessary to return to Newcastle.

Talking to a number of Norwegians who lived near the fjord in the war, it became apparent that Beaufort serial AW200 must have broken up more than we realised, and was thus no longer recognisable as an aeroplane shape. Among the many parts recovered during the war were the cupola of the turret and the pilot's instrument panel. The latter was taken out into the fjord and sunk, to deny it to the Germans. It seems that a properly equipped survey vessel would be required to carry out a search for the remains.

At 13.00 hours local time (11.00 hours GMT) on 13 August 1991, about 200 people gathered at the memorial site for the unveiling ceremony. The King of

Hawker Siddeley Nimrod MR2 serial XV233 of No. 42 (Torpedo Bomber) Squadron, which flew under low cloud to commemorate the ceremony at Bömlo in Norway on 13 August 1991. *(No. 42 (Torpedo Bomber) Squadron)*

Norway was represented by the county governor, Per Skulsted, and the British Embassy by the naval attaché, Commander George Pearson OBE, RN. Eighteen relatives of the crew of AW200 were present, as well as a number of veterans from the Norwegian Air Force and the RAF. The RAF sub-aqua team also attended.

The ceremony began with an address by the deputy mayor, Oyvind Halleraker. Somewhat to my surprise, I had been asked to follow on with another address and then to have the honour of unveiling the plaque on the stone monument. It was pouring with rain and as many of the gathering as possible were sheltering under umbrellas. Soon after I began my short address, a four-engined aircraft came out of the low cloud in the far distance on my right, just for a second or two, and then disappeared. It was Nimrod MR2 serial XV233 of No. 42 (Torpedo Bomber) Squadron, and the captain was Squadron Leader Ian Coleman.

At precisely the appointed time, 13.15. hours, the Nimrod appeared under the dark grey cloud, flying slowly and steadily at about 1,200 feet over the site. I was at the point of finishing my address before moving to the memorial stone, and was able to explain the purpose of the flypast to the crowd. The atmosphere was already emotional, and for some relatives the sight of this graceful machine was almost overwhelming.

There was a short service after the unveiling, followed by the British National Anthem. The commemoration closed with the laying of wreaths, and then the guests reassembled for lunch with the Bömlo Council. No. praise can be too high for the welcome afforded by these open-hearted Norwegians.

Another group of veterans had also gathered to commemorate 13 August 1941, for it was on that night that thirty-one patriotic and courageous young Norwegians had set off from Böröy fjord in a small fishing boat, bound for the Shetlands to join the Allied forces. They told us that the attacks made on Haugesund by the Beauforts had diverted the attention of the German patrol craft and enabled the group of patriots to make good their escape.

The men of the RAF sub-aqua team were disappointed in the result of their efforts but they learnt a great deal from their experiences, and a report was prepared for the benefit of any future expeditions to Norway. Since a close connection had been established with this group of tough, resourceful and skilled men, it seemed likely that I would be involved with some of their future exploits.

At the end of December 1941 the first of the Beaufort squadrons, No. 22, was withdrawn from UK service for operations at Singapore. The aircraft flew from

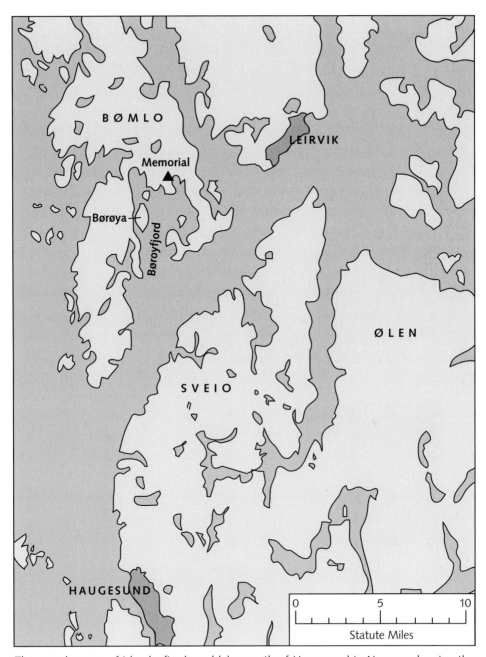

The complex area of islands, fjords and lakes north of Haugesund in Norway, showing the position of the memorial to four RAF men of No. 42 Squadron RAF.

Portreath in Cornwall to Gibraltar and then refuelled for the dangerous passage to Malta before continuing to the Middle East. The ground crews were despatched on the long sea journey. But Malaya was lost to the Japanese before these moves could be completed. Instead, the aircraft remained in Egypt for a

A general view of the locality, looking towards Böröy fjord. *(Flight Sergeant Ian MacKay)*

A Norwegian 'Shetland bus' en route to Britain, photographed in the North Sea on 22 September 1941 from a Beaufort of No. 42 Squadron. The crew and passengers in this fishing boat waved delightedly when they saw the RAF roundels. One man became so excited that he fell overboard and had to be fished out by the others. The photograph was taken with an F24 camera mounted vertically, with a mirror giving an oblique shot to the rear. The tailwheel of the Beaufort is in the photograph, which has been enlarged. *(Flight Lieutenant N. Boynton RAFVR)*

few weeks and were then despatched to Ceylon to help counter the menace of the Japanese fleet which was threatening the Indian Ocean.

In the early summer of 1942 all three remaining Beaufort squadrons in the UK were also ordered overseas. The first was No. 217 Squadron, which left in early June for Ceylon. Most aircraft reached Malta, where they were retained for operations from this beleaguered island fortress. Two detachments of No. 86 Squadron followed in July, in order to join No. 217 Squadron in attacks against Axis convoys supplying German and Italian forces in North Africa.

There was already a Beaufort squadron in the Middle East. This was No. 39 Squadron, which had begun to receive these machines in August 1941 when based at Wadi Natrun in Egypt. Nos 39, 86 and 217 Squadrons were formed into an early 'Strike Wing' at Malta, from where they carried out some extremely dangerous operations, sometimes supported by Beaufighter squadrons, at the cost of very heavy casualties.

No. 42 Squadron was the last to be despatched from the UK, and flew out in August 1942. The aircraft reached the Middle East but they and their crews were dispersed to other squadrons instead of operating independently. No. 47 Squadron at Shandur in Egypt converted from Wellesleys in September 1942, forming the last of the RAF's Beaufort squadrons. It received some of the crews and aircraft from No. 42 Squadron and then operated from Egypt. Together with the Beauforts based in Malta, the crews performed prodigies of valour in anti-shipping attacks. These squadrons contributed greatly to interdiction of the enemy's supply route and ultimately to the British victory in the Battle of El Alamein.

After the divers from the RAF Sub-Aqua Association had been thwarted in their attempts to locate the remains of Beaufort I serial AW200 in Böröy fjord during August 1991, they became determined to demonstrate their abilities with another Beaufort. Looking through their records, they noticed that in 1977 a team of RAF divers had investigated a Beaufort on the sea bed off Valletta in Malta, but without identifying the serial number or discovering the reasons which caused the aircraft to ditch. The RAFS-AA proposed sending a team to Malta, and meanwhile asked me to carry out research on the Beauforts which were lost from the famous George Cross Island. In early 1992 they appointed their Special Projects Officer, Master Engineer Phil Nobbs of No. 10 Squadron at Brize Norton, as Expedition Leader. Phil set about the long and difficult task of oranising the expedition, which was named 'Operation Beaufort' by the RAF. He was presented with the problem that the Beaufort might be a War Grave and therefore should be left untouched. It was also possible that there might be a torpedo underneath the machine, presenting a serious hazard to the divers.

Beaufort IA of No. 217 Squadron in a blast pen at Luqa in Malta. This Mark was fitted with two Vickers 0.303 inch machine-guns in the nose, operated by the navigator, as well as a Yagi aerial for the Air to Surface-Vessel Mark II radar under the nose. The photograph was taken shortly before the aircraft took off on 20 June 1942, flown by Flying Officer F. John R.T. Minster. It was in combat with Junkers Ju88s near Sicily and shot down, but the position where it crashed into the sea is not known. *(Author's collection)*

Another of the prime movers in the project was Frederick Galea of the National War Museum Association in Valletta. This museum, built in the Fort St Elmo which is renowned for the epic defence of the Knights of Malta against the invading Turks in 1565, contains exhibits from the no less heroic defence of the Maltese and the British against the assaults of the Axis powers during the Second World War. Of course, these exhibits include many examples from the air war over Malta, both in the defence of the island and in the offensive operations carried out against Italian air bases and enemy convoys supplying the Axis forces in North Africa.

The discovery of the Beaufort in 1977 came about in a rather unusual manner. The captain of a converted minesweeper, Jim Griffiths, was in Malta on business and having his hair cut in Sliema when the barber mentioned that he had seen a Beaufort crash into the sea during 1942. He was able to give a very accurate position of the downed aircraft. Jim Griffiths located the aircraft with an echo sounder, and a dive took place which confirmed that it was indeed a Bristol Beaufort. This information was passed on to the RAF (Malta) Sub-Aqua

Club, for at the time there was still an RAF presence on the island. The National War Museum Association was also contacted. Frederick Galea (non-diver) and James Farrugia (diver) combined forces with an RAF team to carry out a joint survey.

The Beaufort lay about 450 yards off shore at a depth of about 95 feet. The first dive took place from a patrol boat on 31 August 1977. The purpose was primarily photographic and it was discovered that visibility at the bottom was satisfactory, although not excellent. The Beaufort proved to be without its rear fuselage and tail unit, while the nose had broken up. The two engines had come away from the wings but were lying nearby, with their undercarriage legs still attached. Some of the remainder of the aircraft was buried in sand, which rose in clouds when disturbed, but the divers were able to enter the fuselage. They found a box which came away easily from its mountings and they brought it to the surface tied to a rope. It proved to be an Air to Surface-Vessel Mark II radar, and it was cleaned of its accretions and put on display in the museum.

The second dive took place a fortnight later, and the team took a 45 gallon drum for lifting purposes, attached by a chain to the patrol boat. They came across the turret, together with its twin machine-guns, lying some distance from the fuselage. A spare set of compressed air cylinders had been let into the drum, which they tied to the turret before releasing the air. But this lifting apparatus proved insufficiently buoyant, until the guns and their mounting suddenly broke loose from the turret and shot to the surface, together with the drum. On the surface, it was discovered that they were Browning 0.303 inch, encrusted with barnacles. Belts of live ammunition, dated 1941, were still attached. These guns were cleaned in the RAF's armourer's shop at Luqa and put on display in the museum.

The third dive was made on 22 September 1977, when the team took five drums with them in the hope of recovering an engine and an undercarriage leg. These were attached by shackles to an engine, but it refused to budge when the compressed air was released. It was necessary to return to shore and collect three more drums, and with the aid of this extra buoyancy the engine and leg rose to the surface. They were towed to shore, where heavy recovery vehicles were waiting. Unfortunately these relics deteriorated badly and after some years they were junked.

This was the extent of my knowledge in early 1992 when I began my researches at the Public Record Office and also corresponded with Frederick Galea as well as other interested parties. There were several questions to try to resolve. What was the mark and serial number of the Beaufort? When had it come down in the sea? Was there a torpedo underneath the fuselage? Above all,

A diver sitting on the turret seat in 1977, with another diver approaching on the right.
(Flight Lieutenant Graham Fairhurst RAF (Ret'd))

what had happened to the crew and should the machine be classified as a War Grave?

Of course, I knew that three marks of Beaufort had flown from Malta during 1942, and that each possessed certain distinguishing features. The first was the Mark I, which was fitted with Taurus engines and carried either one or two Vickers K guns in the turret. The second was the Mark IA, which was also powered by Taurus engines but was fitted with a Blenheim type turret containing two Brownings plus two free-handling Vickers guns in the nose, operated by the navigator. The third was the Mark IIA, with two Twin Wasp engines, the Blenheim type turret with the two Brownings and the two Vickers in the nose.

It was obvious from the Brownings that the relic must be either a Mark IA or a Mark IIA, but when I asked Frederick Galea for the type of engine recovered, it transpired that no record had been kept. Numerous Beauforts had been lost from Malta and it seemed impossible to make an identification, even after whittling down some of the numerous possibilities.

One member of the original team of divers had retired from the RAF. This was Flight Lieutenant Graham Fairhurst, who was able to tell me that during a later dive one of the propellers had been recovered. This could provide a further clue, for the propellers of Taurus engines were different from those of the Twin Wasp. Disappointingly, Frederick Galea told me that after being brought up from the salt water of the Mediterranean the buckled propeller had deteriorated rapidly and had also been junked. But then he made an important discovery, for he spotted the propeller in a photograph he had taken, standing against a wall in a yard. This showed that it had the right-hand (or clockwise rotation) of the Taurus engine, whereas the Twin Wasp propeller turned in the other direction. Thus the relic must be a Beaufort IA, eliminating the more numerous Mark IIAs. I began to feel that there might be a chance of making a positive identification.

Fortunately for air historians and those of us who served in Beaufort squadrons, a book entitled *The Beaufort File* was compiled by Roger Hayward after about twenty years of diligent research and published by Air Britain in 1990. This shows in very brief form the fate of every Beaufort built in Britain and Australia. Those produced in the latter country were slightly different from the British Beauforts, the first Mark IIs entering service in February 1942. They were employed on shipping strikes in the Pacific theatre and later versions were fitted with increased armament and used for strafing ground targets.

Roger and I worked independently through all the Beaufort IA entries, eliminating those where the aircraft were known to have come down elsewhere or where survivors in our Beaufort Aircrews Association were able to provide further information. Our resulting lists showed the same eight possible aircraft.

My next move was to visit the Air Historical Branch (RAF) in London and ask a member of the staff to examine these eight possibilities in their casualty reports. His information eliminated four and indicated that two others were no more than very remote possibilities. This left me with two main possibilities. Meanwhile further evidence had arrived from Graham Fairhurst, for the control column had also been brought up several years before. Although this had since been junked, a photograph showed an ominous nick in the spectacle which looked as though it had been caused by a bullet. In addition, Graham remembered that the engine which had been brought up showed signs of a fire.

The first of the two remaining possibilities was Beaufort IA serial DD959 of No. 217 Squadron, which was lost on 20 June 1942. Early in that month, the aircrews of this squadron began their flights to Ceylon. Nine Beauforts flew out via Gibraltar and arrived at Luqa on 10 June, where they were eagerly seized by HQ Malta as a gift from the gods. Six more arrived the following day, and nine of these fifteen aircraft were despatched to attack the Italian Fleet on 15 June. One of these torpedoed and sank the heavy cruiser *Trento* and caused the remaining warships to turn back from their intended attack against an Allied convoy. Thereafter the Beauforts were thrown against Axis convoys again and again, sinking many ships but suffering heavy losses themselves.

Beaufort IA serial DD959, flown by Flying Officer F. John R.T. Minster, was sent out on one of these occasions, on 20 June, with eleven other aircraft of No. 217 Squadron and an escort of eight Beaufighters of No. 235 Squadron, to attack an enemy convoy off Sicily. Two Beauforts took off late, owing to engine trouble. These were flown by John Minster and Sergeant Jimmy Hutcheson, and the pair tried to catch up with the main formation. When they arrived off Sicily they were attacked by four Junkers Ju88 long-distance fighters, coloured black, from I./*Nachtjagdgeschwader* 2. Hutcheson jettisoned his torpedo and an air battle ensued for 35 minutes, with two of these Ju88s making a series of attacks on his Beaufort. One enemy aircraft was hit by return fire and turned for Sicily, emitting smoke, where it landed safely. But the other Junkers followed the Beaufort almost to Malta before clearing off. Nobody saw what happened to Minster, and he and his crew have no known grave.

Hutcheson was killed a fortnight later, with a different crew, but two of his original crew were members of the Beaufort Aircrews Association. It seemed to us possible that Minister might have managed to ditch near Valletta, with one engine on fire and a bullet through the spectacle of his control column. But there was no reference to this in any of the RAF records, and it seemed unlikely that he could have reached this position without an entry of some sort, for the ditching would have been seen from the shore and duly reported.

The most likely possibility for the ditched aircraft was one in transit as part of No. 1 Overseas Aircraft Despatch Unit. This had flown out from Portreath in Cornwall to Gibraltar and then Malta, en route for Egypt in order to join No. 42 Squadron. It was Beaufort IA serial DW805, flown by Pilot Officer Ernest Moody, which took off from Luqa at 07.50 hours on 21 August 1942 and came down in the sea near Valletta shortly afterwards, after the port engine had failed. According to its Accident Card at the RAF Museum, the constant speed unit failed and the propeller went into fully fine pitch, so that Moody could not maintain height. He was complimented on his 'good effort' in making the ditching. It seemed possible that the fire in the port engine might have been cuased by an electrical spark or by the fracture of a fuel pipe, and that the nick in the control column might have been abrasion from a shackle when it was raised to the surface. The four crew members were picked up by high speed launch, with the wireless operator Sergeant Owen Pritchard slightly injured. The records do not give the names of the other two crew members at the time, but a member of the Beaufort Aircrews Association remembered that Sergeant Griffiths was the navigator and Sergeant S. Gill was the gunner.

With these researches at an end, there remained the overriding question. How could the RAF team identify the aircraft under water? Roger Hayward made the excellent suggestion that they should look for one of the small manufacturer's metal plates which were fitted to all RAF aircraft, usually painted over. But we did not know the positions of these, for no example of a British-built Beaufort existed.

By this time, a Beaufort IIA had been rebuilt by Hawkins of Texas and put on display in December 1941 by the Royal Air Force Museum at Hendon. But this was not a reliable guide, for it was put together from parts found in Australia and New Guinea. But an examination of the Bristol Beaufighter in the RAF Museum was made, in the expectation that the positions would be the same as those on a Bristol Beaufort. One plate was found under the starboard tailplane and one under each wing, outboard of the engine and in front of the flaps. It was believed that there was another plate on the starboard nose, but we could not clamber up to that position.

After all these investigations, I prepared a portfolio for the RAF team, containing 'cutaway' diagrams of Beauforts, photographs and details of Mark IAs and a short list of the possible aircraft. I must confess to a feeling of nervousness in case this long process of elimination had produced the wrong result. Then a copy of an article was sent to me from Malta, in the June 1992 issue of the Italian magazine *SUB*. I translated this rather slowly and learnt that two divers from Malta, Derek Chircop and Raymond Ciancio, had also been down on the machine. The Italian author of the article described the relic quite accurately, but asserted that it was Beaufort I serial W6498. A quick check enabled me to establish that this machine had never flown overseas but had been 'struck off charge' on 27 September 1945, at RAF Crosby-on-Eden in Cumberland.

Meanwhile Phil Nobbs had been beavering away with the even more difficult job of assembling his team and making a myriad of arrangements. He wrote nearly 100 letters, primarily asking for financial support, and received a handful of favourable replies. However, the bulk of the cost was borne by the RAF team members, who contributed £260 each plus their own incidental expenses. It was found less expensive to make package arrangements with travel agents than to pay for air fares, and then hire tents in Malta. The final Administration Order consisted of nine pages, signed by the Officer Commanding RAF Brize Norton. Six months had elapsed since the project had been proposed.

The RAF sub-aqua team finally left Gatwick for Malta on 11 October 1992. It consisted of twelve divers armed with photographs, drawings and an array of information, as well as their weighty equipment. They were Squadron Leader John Sadler from Henlow, Flight Lieutenant Mark Istance from Leuchars, Master Engineer Phil Nobbs from Brize Norton, Warrant Officer Dave

Whitehall from Kinloss, Chief Technician Chris Manning from Chivenor, Sergeant Ian Woodcock from St Mawgan, Sergeant Martin Marle from Kinloss, Sergeant Al Murrie from Lossiemouth, Corporal Reg Banks from Brize Norton, Corporal Andy King from Coltishall, Corporal Al Middlemiss from Finningly and Senior Aircraftman Roy Hemmings from Chivenor. They were joined by two civilian divers, Flight Lieutenant Graham Fairhurst RAF (Ret'd) and a lady from Oxfordshire, Jo Reilly, both at their own expense.

All the servicemen were reminded that they were on duty for the entire period of the expedition. Their aims were to identify the Beaufort, to bring up the two forward-firing Vickers guns in the navigator's position for the National War Museum of Malta, to survey the area, to take extensive photographs, and to gain practical experience. Advance publicity had been given to the expedition, and poignant letters arrived from relatives and friends of Beaufort men who had failed to return, hoping for positive news after all those years. None of these letters contained names of the crew members of our two main possibilities.

The diving began almost immediately after reporting to the British High Commission in Malta. Frederick Galea had arranged for Dive Systems of Malta to provide the converted lifeboat *Birzee Queen* at a discount, while other Maltese concerns had helped to sponsor the trips. The whole team caried out a preliminary reconnaissance dive to familiarise themselves with the aircraft and to formulate a plan of attack. They found that the machine lay in 97 feet of water, giving only sixteen minutes of work time on the bottom without the danger of suffering the effects of decompression.

They decided to concentrate on the trailing edges of both wings, hoping to tunnel underneath and locate the maker's plates which were known to be stamped with the serial number of the aircraft. For safety reasons, the divers worked in 'buddy pairs'. This task was carried out with the aid of an air lift pump, an 'underwater vacuum cleaner' which could remove the sand. After many dives and extracting over half a ton of sand, a diver was just able to squeeze underneath each wing and extend an arm to feel for one of the plates. But the sand kept sliding back and neither of these plates was found.

Unfortunately the weather proved stormy, with accompanying seas which were so rough that work was hampered for several days. Nevertheless the divers made several discoveries. It became evident that the Beaufort had struck the top of a reef, destroying the nose and leaving a trail of wreckage as it careered forward. The rear fuselage and tail unit had broken off and must have drifted away, for this part was never located. Part of the Yagi aerial under the nose was discovered and brought up. It was clear that other divers had been down on the wreck, for a piece of the fuselage had disappeared and the remainder was strung

The converted lifeboat *Birzee Queen* hired by the RAF Sub-Aqua Team in 1992, with Corporal Reg Banks ashore and Louis Scriberras of Dive Systems Malta in the bow. *(Master Engineer Phil Nobbs)*

The Browning machine-gun in the starboard wing of the Beaufort, with Master Engineer Phil Nobbs (left) and Senior Aircraftman Roy Hemmings chiselling off the retaining rings. *(Warrant Officer Dave Whitehall)*

Master Engineer Phil Nobbs holding the ammunition box for the Browning machine-gun after removal from the starboard wing. *(Warrant Officer Dave Whitehall)*

with ropes and 45 gallon drums, apparently placed in a vain effort to raise the machine.

The two Vickers 0.303 inch machine-guns in the nose had disappeared, confirming the belief that the aircraft had struck a reef in its descent. A pair of divers searched this reef and found a long metal object encrusted in the rock. It was brought to the surface and identified as the barrel of one of these guns. The divers also managed to remove and bring up the Browning machine-gun in the starboard wing, but quickly dumped the ammunition back in the sea when the rounds began to fizz ominously. The gun was found to be in good condition and it was handed to Frederick Galea, who sometimes accompanied the team. After some treatment, it was even possible to move the breechlock.

Attempts to locate the manufacturer's plates proved fruitless, for those under the wings could not be reached while those on the rear fuselage and the nose were not present. Each diver could stay at that depth for a total of only about one hour a day, and only thirteen days were available. The men began to wonder if they could make a positive identification.

After eight days of work, Phil Nobbs decided to switch the air lift pump to the interior of the Beaufort, which was buried in about three feet of sand. This was difficult work, for only one diver could enter the fuselage at one time while the action of the air pump caused the sand to rise in clouds and reduce visibility to nil. The divers worked blind by scooping the sand towards the nozzle, feeling for any objects and placing them in their recovery bags. About 150 small items were recoverd in this way, including items of kit from behind the pilot's seat. One of these was a Lee Enfield 0.38 inch revolver, another was the shoulder tab of a pilot officer and another was the brass eagle from an officer's forage cap. But the most important of all was a hairbrush, which had lost its bristles but had a pre-war airman's number stamped on it.

I had intended to join the team during their second week, but pressure of other commitments prevented my visit. As things turned out, this was providential. Phil Nobbs telephoned me in the evening, giving me this number, for I had prepared a list of all potential aircrew members with their service numbers. To our acute disappointment, it corresponded with none of these. But about an hour later I suddenly realised what it could be. Many RAF officers were non-commissioned during their early training and were issued with an airman's kit. It was normal to stamp or to ink service numbers on this kit, as some protection against light-fingered comrades in the barrack blocks. Items such as brushes were not handed back when a commission arrived.

Could this hairbrush show the service number of Pilot Officer Ernest Moody before he was commissioned? A telephone call the next morning to the Air Historical Branch – for this was a service project and not a civilian matter – verified that my guess was correct. When Phil telephoned me the following evening, I was able to pass on this exhilarating information. A fax congratulating the team was sent by the Air Historical Branch (RAF) to the British High Commission in Malta. The relic was not a War Grave, since the crew had been rescued. There was no torpedo lying underneath, for the bomb bay of Beauforts on delivery to the Middle East carried a large auxiliary fuel tank.

The RAF team completed all they could in the remaining time. Their last action was to strip the Beaufort of all ropes and drums and to raise the Union Jack above its radio aerial. They returned home on Sunday 25 October 1992.

However, soon after they departed another team of divers descended on the Beaufort. They must have been watching the proceedings and waiting for an opportunity. Despite the Antiquities Protection Act of the Maltese Government, they attempted to tow the Beaufort to shallow water off St Paul's Bay, where it could be viewed by tourists in glass-bottomed boats. The aircraft broke up in the winter gales and is no longer recognisable.

This was not the end of the story, for an examination of the RAF Retired List showed the name of Squadron Leader Ernest Moody. Further enquiries located him at his home in Cornwall and it was decided to arrange a presentation of some of the artifacts recovered from the Beaufort. This took place on 2 October 1993 at the Mary Rose Club in RAF St Mawgan, near Newquay. Ernest

Flight Lieutenant Mark Istance with the hairbrush he found behind the pilot's seat of the Beaufort, bearing service no. 565285. *(Ms Jo Reilly)*

Master Engineer Phil Nobbs, the expedition leader, with his diving helmet and breathing mouthpiece removed almost 100 feet below the surface, saluting the Union Flag and the Beaufort relic at the end of the diving. *(Warrant Officer Dave Whitehall)*

Squadron Leader Ernest Moody presented with some of his lost effects after more than fifty years – hat badge, fork and spoon, and hairbrush. Front row, left to right: Corporal Reg Banks; Chief Technician Chris Manning; Squadron Leader Ernest Moody; Master Engineer Phil Nobbs; Squadron Leader John Sadler. Back row: Senior Aircraftman Roy Hemmings; Sergeant Ian Woodcock; Warrant Officer Dave Whitehall; Ms Jo Reilly. *(The late Squadron Leader Norman Hearn-Phillips AFC, DFM)*

Moody and some of his family were collected and about thirty-five members of the RAF Sub-Aqua Association were present, as well as their guests. These included eight of the group which had been on the dive off Valletta.

A video of the dive was shown and Ernest Moody was then reunited with the badge from his forage cap, mounted in a plaque. Other articles presented to him included his knife, fork and spoon with which all airmen were issued, plus of course his hairbrush stamped with his airman's number. We learned that he had begun his RAF career as a boy apprentice at Halton but had later qualified for pilot training.

Ernest Moody confirmed that the port engine of Beaufort IA serial DD959 had failed soon after take-off from Luqa, bound for No. 42 Squadron at Landing Ground 228 in Egypt, and he had no option but to put the heavily laden machine down in the sea. Sergeant Gill was the wireless operator, and he managed to release the H Type dinghy in the port wing. Moody and his navigator, Sergeant Griffiths, were also unharmed. The only minor casualty was Sergeant Pritchard in the turret, who gashed his knee.

The four men were picked up from their dingy by an RAF launch and later flown to Egypt in a Dakota. They rejoined No. 42 Squadron in October 1942 when it was re-established in Ceylon. In February 1943, the squadron was re-equipped with Blenheim Vs, known as Bisleys, and then moved to Rajyeswarpur in India, from where it began flying bomber missions over the Burma Front. After the war, Ernest Moody took a permanent commission in the RAF.

The occasion at the Mary Rose Club was attended by newspaper reporters and a TV cameraman. It was a very convivial meeting, as well as a fitting conclusion to the successful expedition to Malta by the RAF Sub-Aqua Association.

CHAPTER FOUR

The Duke of Kent

Short Sunderland III, letter M serial W4026 of No. 228 Squadron, began to take off from Invergordon in the Cromarty Firth at 13.10 hours British Double Summer Time on Tuesday 25 August 1942, on a flight to Iceland. About half an hour later the flying boat crashed on Eagle's Rock, 700 feet above sea level, three miles inland from Dunbeath in Caithness and at an angle of about 15°W of its intended track. All those on board were killed except the rear gunner.

Such a flying accident, one of hundreds which occurred in the hills and mountains of Scotland during the war, would have gone unremarked by air historians and journalists if it were not for a single factor: one of the passengers was HRH Air Commodore the Duke of Kent, KG, KT, GCMG, GCVO, the fourth son of HM King George V and the youngest brother of the reigning monarch, HM King George VI. Since then there have been several accounts of the crash, some theorising about a 'cover-up'. However, when I was asked to make an independent analysis of the crash by the editor of *Aeroplane Monthly*, it became apparent that these accounts had made few attempts to put the readers in the positions of the Sunderland aircrew or to explain the tragedy by referring to the equipment on board and possible errors in navigational procedures.

The purpose of the flight was primarily non-operational, in order to carry the Duke of Kent to Iceland, where he intended to tour RAF stations in his role as Inspector-General of RAF Welfare. In May 1940, British forces had entered Iceland, which was then a self-governing state under the King of Denmark, partly to forestall any landing which the Germans might attempt after their invasion of Denmark and Norway. The island was very valuable for RAF air bases, from which protection could be afforded to convoys passing through a swathe of the North Atlantic. Reykjavik harbour could be used by flying boats, with attendant facilities nearby, while there was an airfield available near the port. Coastal Command's No. 18 Group had begun work on airfields in August 1940, and RAF facilities were set up at Kaldadarnes, Budareyri and Akureyri.

The Duke of Kent's itinerary was scheduled to include visits to naval and army establishments as well as RAF units. In July 1941, American forces had begun to relieve the British Army of the task of garrisoning the country, and the Duke of Kent also intended to pay goodwill visits to US Army units. Many Icelanders were unhappy with the enforced occupation of their country, perhaps understandably. The Duke hoped to improve the unfriendly atmosphere in which the Allied servicemen lived.

Iceland provided a transit point for aircraft flying between Canada and Britain, and in addition it enabled Coastal Command aircraft to patrol south-east towards the Faeroes to search for U-boats sailing between their bases in Norway and their hunting areas in the Atlantic. Many RAF aircraft flying to and from Iceland carried depth charges and the crews kept a constant look-out for U-boats. Sunderland W4026 was no exception, being equipped with eight 250lb depth charges. These were suspended from carriages within the bomb bay, ready to be winched out under the wings before any action, through bomb doors in the sides of the hull.

The aircraft was fitted with Mark II air-to-surface vessel (ASV) radar which could pick up U-boats on the surface, and the airmen were under orders to attack if they made a contact. This was in spite of the presence of the Duke of Kent, who in any event was a serving RAF officer and thus 'on active service'. Although his role was non-operational, he was subject to some of the hazards of war. Normally, the attacking aircraft was spotted before reaching the U-boat, which then crash-dived. Such attacks could be less dangerous than other RAF operations at that stage of the war. It was not until the following year that *Grossadmiral* Karl Doenitz ordered his U-boat crews to stay on the surface and fight it out with attacking aircraft.

Sunderland W4026 had been serviced and repainted at Oban prior to the flight. It was a fairly new machine, having been 'taken on charge' by No. 228 Squadron in the middle of the previous May. The colour for Sunderlands by that time was 'Coastal White', except for the plan-view upper surfaces, which were camouflaged in dark slate-grey and extra dark sea-grey. The squadron letters DQ had been dropped but the aircraft letter M was painted on the sides of the hull in dark slate-grey, together with the RAF roundels outlined in yellow. The serial W4026 was in black. On the nose, a squadron artist had painted a Disney-like picture of a female kangaroo with her young in her pouch, both wearing boxing gloves, to symbolise the Australians who served in No. 228 Squadron. The machine had been rigged up as a VIP aircraft, even to the extent of curtains in the windows, and had already been used to transport high-ranking officers of the Royal Navy to the Hebrides and coastal bases in west Scotland.

There were four passengers in the royal party. The first was the Duke of Kent, age thirty-nine, who was married to Princess Marina. He had spent several years

Sunderland III, letters NS:Z serial ML824 of No. 201 Squadron, taking off. This flying boat is now on display in the Battle of Britain Hall of the Royal Air Force Museum at Hendon. *(Brian Hansley collection)*

The flight deck of a Sunderland, with the first pilot at the controls while the second pilot signals to a convoy with an Aldis lamp. *(Author's collection)*

The kangaroo mascot on Sunderland III letter M serial W4026 of No. 228 Squadron. *(Joe Ayling/John Evans collection)*

The Duke of Kent in RAF tropical uniform in 1941. *(Author's collection)*

of his youth in the Royal Navy and between the wars had worked in both the Foreign Office and the Home Office. He was highly intelligent and widely read, being well-informed in the arts, especially music and antiques. In April 1940 he had been appointed as a staff officer in the RAF's Training Command and chose the function of RAF welfare as his wartime career, even though this carried a lower rank. He was genuinely interested in improving the living conditions of RAF aircrews and ground personnel. He was well liked for his warmth and charm of manner, and frequently visited RAF stations, with as little formality as possible. During the previous summer, he had made a flight to Canada, in order to study conditions in the Empire Air Training Scheme which was expanding rapidly in that country. He had also visited US air stations which were training RAF pilots.

Accompanying the Duke was his private secretary, Lieutenant John A. Lowther, MVO, RNVR; he was aged thirty-one, grandson and heir to Viscount

Group Captain the Duke of Kent (centre) visiting No. 8 Bombing and Air Gunnery School at Evanton in Ross-shire on 13 May 1941. *(Brian Hansley collection)*

Ullswater, a former Speaker of the House of Commons. The air equerry was Pilot Officer the Hon. C.V. Michael Strutt, RCAF, age twenty-seven, who had enlisted as an air gunner; he was a son of Lord Belper and brother of the Duchess of Norfolk, and had taken the place of Squadron Leader Peter J. Ferguson, who was unwell. The fourth member of the party was the Duke's batman, Leading Aircraftman John W. Hales, RAFVR, age twenty-five, from Norfolk.

There was a mixture of flying experience in the crew of the Sunderland. The captain was an Australian in the RAF, Flight Lieutenant Frank M. Goyen, age twenty-five, from Shepparton in the state of Victoria. He had travelled to Britain in 1938 and successfully applied for a short-service commission in the RAF. His flying log book included 906 hours in Sunderlands, and he was thus nearing the end of his tour with No. 228 Squadron. Much of his flying had taken place in the Mediterranean, operating from such bases as Gibraltar, Alexandria, and Kalafrana in Malta. These had included some dangerous incidents. More recently, he had flown over the North Atlantic from No. 228 Squadron's base at Oban in Argyll. During his flying he had made several attacks on U-boats, although he had claimed none of these as 'probables'. He had flown in No. 228 Squadron for almost two years and was highly respected as a man with a careful and precise approach to flying, being admired for his courage as well as his skill.

Goyen's second pilot was Pilot Officer Sydney W. Smith, an Australian in the RAAF, age twenty-four, who had volunteered in early 1940 when employed by the Water Board and living near Sydney. He was a fairly experienced pilot, having made a number of operational flights, but only the last three with Goyen. The navigator was Pilot Officer George R. Saunders RAFVR, age thirty-one, from Sheffield. According to the squadron operations record book, he had made only three operational flights, all of which were with Goyen although two were under tuition as a second navigator. His place in the crew came about as a matter of luck. Flight Lieutenant Archie Brember, the squadron navigation officer, had been detailed for the flight to Iceland, for Goyen was without his regular navigator, but such was the competition to fly in the VIP aircraft that the other navigators had protested. They were allowed to draw lots and Saunders was the navigator who picked the 'winning ticket'.

All the NCOs were part of Goyen's regular crew. There were three wireless operator/air gunners. Sergeant Edward F. Blacklock, age thirty, had joined the RNZAF soon after the outbreak of war. Sergeant Arthur R. Catt, age twenty-four, was a pre-war airman from Enfield in Middlesex. Lastly, Flight Sergeant

The Duke of Kent at Mount Batten in Devon on 15 February 1942, talking to Flight Lieutenant Roger E. 'Tiny' Hunter DFC of No. 240 Squadron. This squadron was based at Castle Archdale in Northern Ireland and equipped with Catalina Is. At 6ft 8in, Roger Hunter was reputed to be the tallest pilot in the RAF. He later served with No. 422 (RCAF) Squadron, which was equipped with Catalinas and then Sunderlands. (*Squadron Leader Roger E. Hunter via John Evans*)

Andrew S.W. Jack, age twenty-one, was a Scotsman from Grangemouth in Stirling who had joined the RAFVR after the outbreak of war. There were four fitters, all of whom were pre-war airmen. Flight Sergeant William R. Jones, age twenty-eight, who was also qualified as an air gunner, came from Port Talbot in Glamorganshire. Flight Sergeant Charles N. Lewis, age twenty-seven, was an airframe fitter from Letterston in Pembrokeshire. Flight Sergeant Ernest J. Hewerdine, age twenty-four, was a wireless electrical mechanic who had also qualified as an air gunner, and came from Grantham in Lincolnshire. Finally, Sergeant Leonard E. Sweett, age twenty-two, was from Looe in Cornwall.

The commanding officer of No. 228 Squadron had decided to accompany his crew and the royal party on the flight. He was Wing Commander Thomas L. Moseley, aged twenty-nine, from Tamworth in Staffordshire. He had entered Cranwell in September 1931 and graduated as a pilot officer in July 1933. Most of his RAF career, up to the autumn of 1937, had been on flying boats based at Malta. Then he had concentrated on navigation and had become an instructor at the School of Air Navigation at Manston in Kent. Before taking over command of No. 228 Squadron on 30 April 1942, he had spent a year on the staff of the Deputy Director of Training at the Air Ministry, and had then taken a fortnight's conversion course on Sunderlands with No. 4 (Coastal) Operational Training Unit, which was based at Stranraer with a detachment at Invergordon.

By 25 August 1942, Moseley had completed 1,449 hours of flying, but with only 81 hours in Sunderlands, most of these in company with Goyen, and so far he had made no flights as captain. His position in this last flight is recorded as first pilot. However, it is probable that, although he would have taken turns at the controls, his primary function was to act as host to the royal party. He must have been keen to demonstrate the flying characteristics of the prestigious Sunderland, which was a military version of the Imperial Airways flying boat, and to explain the latest equipment. The Duke of Kent was also a pilot and would have been interested in such matters.

The Sunderland took off from Oban at 15.35 hours on Sunday 23 August for the flight to Invergordon, to await further orders. The Duke of Kent and his small entourage arrived by rail from London during the evening of the following day.

On Tuesday 25 August the officer members of the crew, including Wing Commander Moseley, were briefed by the Station Commander of Invergordon, Group Captain Geoffrey Francis. In correspondence with myself, this senior officer explained that he instructed them to keep well clear of the east coast of Scotland and to climb until they had reached a sufficient height to fly above any high ground as well as a patch of bad weather in the area of Wick, before turning to Iceland.

Flight Lieutenant Frank Goyen's crew before his final flight. Top row, left to right: Pilot Officer Douglas V.C. Hammond (who was not on the last flight); Flight Sergeant Andrew S.W. Jack; Flight Sergeant William R. Jones; Sergeant Leonard E. Sweett; Unidentified pilot; Sergeant Arthur R. Catt; Flight Sergeant Charles N. Lewis. Front row: Unidentified navigator; Flight Lieutenant Frank M. Goyen; Flight Sergeant Ernest J. Hewerdine. *(D. Kneale via John Evans)*

The bomb carriages under the wings of Sunderland serial ML824 in the Battle of Britain Hall of the Royal Air Force Museum at Hendon. These carriages were moved to their outboard positions either by an electrical mechanism or manually. These examples are Mark II depth charges, each of 250lb. Sunderland III of No. 228 Squadron was also carrying eight of these depth charges. *(Author's collection)*

The weather for the day is accurately recorded by the National Meteorological Archive at Bracknell, with observations for each region of the British Isles entered at four-hourly intervals. An area of low pressure was centred over Eire, bringing a series of occluded fronts over the whole area. These brought extensive and low stratus cloud to the east coast of Scotland at the time the Sunderland took off, with the base varying from 300 to 2,000 feet. Visibility was poor under the clouds, and there was some coastal fog. The temperature was only about 60° Fahrenheit, but humidity was high and the day was rather muggy. The wind was forecast as somewhat variable, generally from east-south-east at about ten miles per hour. Further to the north, towards the Faeroes, there were breaks in the clouds and better conditions. Although such a summer's day cannot be described as pleasant, Coastal Command crews often flew in conditions which were a great deal worse.

The crew must have gone out to the flying boat about half an hour before the tender brought the royal party and their commanding officer, to prepare for take-off and to welcome their guests as they came on board through the entrance door in the port side. Immediately inside this door were two stairways. One led down to a wardroom on the lower deck, where there were bench seats which could be used as bunks, and a table. It is likely that Leading Aircraftman Hales was sent in this direction, to join those members of the crew who were not required for the early part of the flight. The other stairway led to the commodious flight deck with two seats at the front occupied by the pilots. Behind the captain's seat on the port side was the wireless operator's position, while the navigator sat at his chart table behind the second pilot, from where he had a good field of vision to starboard as well as forward through the pilots' windscreen. It is probable that the Duke of Kent was strapped into the navigator's seat for take-off, while the commanding officer and the other VIPs stood behind the pilots. This was the normal procedure for such passengers in those days.

Laden with the total effective capacity of 2,552 gallons of petrol and 128 gallons of oil, together with 2,000lb of depth-charges and the weight of fifteen men and their gear, the flying boat must have been near its maximum weight of 58,000lb on take-off. The wind was light and the water smooth, without the slightly choppy conditions which favoured an easy take-off. It would have been a long run of about three miles before the aircraft became 'unstuck' and the pilot began a slow climb. According to a report in *The Times*, the flying boat returned and circled over Invergordon. It then set course for the Sutors, the cliffs at the entrance to Cromarty Firth. From here, the normal pinpoint for setting course northwards was the lighthouse at Tarbat Ness, which they would have reached by flying along the low-lying coastline to the north-east. The next logical turning point was to the east of Wick, the RAF airfield which lay in the flat coastal plain of the north-east tip of Scotland. From here the route lay north for a short distance and then north-west over the Pentland Firth between John o'Groats and the Orkneys. The flight across the Atlantic would have been past the Faeroes before making a landfall on the Icelandic coast, and then to Reykjavik. The Sunderland III had a maximum endurance of sixteen hours at an indicated airspeed of 110 knots, and such a flight should have taken no more than seven hours.

Unhappily, the Sunderland was in the air for only about half an hour. A farmer and his son, David and Hugh Morrison, were working on the Duke of Portland's estate near Eagle's Rock, inland from Dunbeath, when they heard the sound of aircraft engines overhead, followed by a shattering explosion. They could see nothing, for the hills were covered with low stratus cloud, but they were in no doubt that there had been a crash, for the smell of burning fuel pervaded the air. Hugh jumped on his motor-bike and rode off to alert the police.

Meanwhile, local people at the small community of Braemore, where the Duke of Portland kept a hunting lodge about two miles from the scene of the crash, had also heard the explosion. The Duke's home of Langwell House in Berriedale was telephoned, and the local postmistress put a call through to Dr John R. Kennedy, a 71-year-old medical officer for the Western District of the Parish of Latheron, who immediately set out by car for Braemore with a small search party he organised. A group of people near Eagle's Rock, including David Morrison, gamekeepers and an innkeeper, had already begun to climb the hills towards the acrid smell of burning fuel. They literally followed their noses, for visibility was no more than about fifteen feet

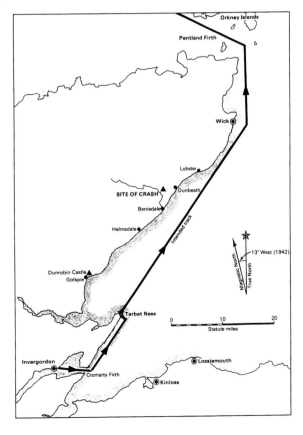

The intended track of Sunderland III serial W4026 of No. 228 Squadron on 25 August 1942.

in the fog-like conditions of the low stratus cloud. The police also set out from Dunbeath.

The first rescuers reached the scene about an hour after the crash. Wreckage, still smouldering, was strewn everywhere. The deep hull of the Sunderland had struck the slope of the hill and the machine had bounced once before turning on its back. The fuel tanks had exploded but the depth-charges had been thrown clear. Bodies were lying on the ground, many badly burned, and all were dead. A special constable found the body of the Duke of Kent, badly mutilated, and identified him from a bracelet on his wrist. This included his address: The Coppins, Iver, Bucks. His monogrammed briefcase lay nearby, burst open, with Icelandic 100 Krona banknotes scattered around.

Dr Kennedy reached the crash site somewhat later and found eleven bodies in and around the wreckage, with three more trapped under burning wreckage. He examined all those accessible and found that death had been caused by multiple injuries and burning. The Duke of Kent's head had been crushed. In his opinion, death in all cases had been instantaneous. He also noticed that the

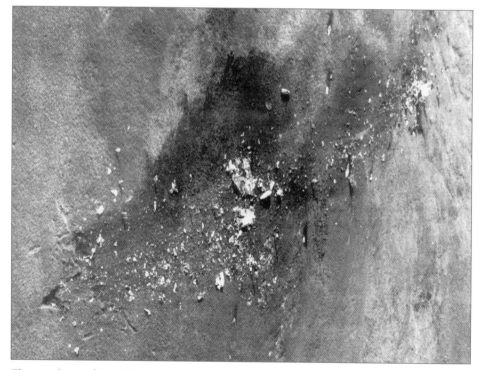

The wreckage of Sunderland III serial W4026 of No. 228 Squadron. The point of impact of the nose, wings and floats can be seen in the bottom left. Then the flying boat somersaulted forwards in a northerly direction, leaving a trail of wreckage and burn marks from the exploding fuel. The floats can be seen in the centre of the photograph, while the tail and the rear turret are in the top right. *(Brian Hansley collection)*

The wreckage of Sunderland III serial W4026 of No. 228 Squadron, photographed from a Lockheed Hudson and viewed towards the south-west. The point of impact is on the left. The tail section, including the rear turret in which Flight Sergeant Andrew Jack survived, is upside down on the right. *(Dave Smith via Hugh Budgen)*

Duke's wristwatch had stopped at 1.42 and, correctly believing that this might provide important evidence, removed it from the body. However, it cannot be assumed that the time indicated by this watch was precisely correct, for the minute hand may have been jarred out of position when the flying boat crashed. Nowadays, such times can often be identified more accurately by 'needle slap', a microscopic examination of the glass, plastic or face of a watch, but this method was not in use at the time. Nevertheless, this time did indicate that the Sunderland had been in the air for about half an hour from its recorded take-off of 13.10 hours from Invergordon, which seems correct.

The rescuers began the sad and gruesome task of taking the bodies down to the neighbouring towns. Not unnaturally, they assumed that everyone on board had died. Unknown to them, however, one man had survived. By the next morning, news of the tragedy had appeared in the newspapers and notifications had been sent to all next-of-kin. One telegram was sent to the widowed mother of the youngest man in the aircraft, Flight Sergeant Andrew W.S. Jack, at her home in Grangemouth. Mrs Jack was out and the telegraph boy was directed to her daughter Jean, who worked in a local office. Jean had read about the crash in the morning newspaper and was already extremely worried for, during a visit a few days before to Andrew at Oban, she and her mother had learnt that he was about to depart on a special flight in a newly serviced Sunderland. She read the telegram and was in acute distress on learning of the 'death' of her brother when another telegram arrived, cancelling the first and stating that Andrew was alive but injured. She was so confused that at first she did not believe the second telegram.

Andrew Jack normally occupied the wireless operator's position, but on this occasion the three NCOs had tossed up for the privilege of being near the royal party, the loser to occupy the rear turret. Jack lost the toss but was unworried, for he was not a man to seek the limelight. As it happened, the coin saved his life for, although the rear turret was usually the most dangerous place during an attack by an enemy fighter, it could be the safest in the event of a crash. When the Sunderland struck the ground and turned over, the rear turret, with its occupant and the four Browning machine guns, broke away from the rear hull, together with the tail-fin and rudder. The gunner, facing backwards, was partly cushioned from the shock of the crash, but he was knocked out and his face, hands and arms were badly burned.

When Jack came to, he staggered round the wreckage and saw the bodies of the crew and the passengers lying on the ground. He thought that he should find help and walked painfully down the hill until he came to the Berriedale river, a few hundred yards away. In the manner of many survivors of air crashes, he followed the river downstream, hoping to find human habitation. His flying boots had been badly damaged and he had to take them off, while his injuries were so severe that he could hobble along only very slowly. At the time he was making his way down the river, the first rescue party was climbing up towards the scene of the crash, and the men did not see the survivor.

After a while, Andrew Jack collapsed into the moss and bracken. He either passed out or went to sleep, for it was late morning of the next day when he regained consciousness. An early morning mist had cleared and the sun was shining, but there was still no sign of habitation. He waded into the river to drink, for he could not use his hands to cup the water. Once more, he carried on down the winding river until fatigue overcame him and he lay down 'to die', as he later told his mother. At this point he heard the sound of a motor car horn and realised that help could not be far away. He got to his feet again and continued until he came across a croft, the home of an elderly couple, Mr and Mrs Sutherland. Opening a gate in the fence with his elbow, he was approaching the door when Mrs Sutherland came out to meet this dreadful apparition, who begged her for a drink. She took him inside, gave him some milk, cut off his pullover, made him as comfortable as she could and rushed off for help.

Meanwhile, the RAF had been active. They asked Captain E.E. Fresson, the captain of a DH Rapide of Scottish Airways, to keep a lookout for the exact position of the crash, which they still did not know accurately. By a strange coincidence, Captain Fresson had flown over Eagle's Rock at the probable time of the crash, while on his way southwards on his regular run from Kirkwall in the Orkneys to Inverness, but had seen nothing through the layer of low stratus cloud beneath. On the earlier part of this flight, he had found Pentland Firth bathed in sunshine.

While Jack was unconscious in the bracken during the following morning, Captain Fresson located the crashed Sunderland, on his flight northwards. He came down to 100 feet and circled. The four Pegasus XVIII engines were scattered around the fragmented wreckage, which had burnt and melted, still smouldering and unrecognisable apart from the tail section which had broken away. Fresson and his radio officer could see three or four bodies which had not yet been taken down the hillside. The RAF's No. 56 Maintenance Unit at Inverness was ordered to clear the wreckage from the hillside, a long task which they completed on 16 September. Even then, some parts of the debris remained on the mountain.

RAF and Admiralty officers had arrived from London to examine the site of the crash, and based themselves at Dr Kennedy's house in Dunbeath. They were sitting down to lunch when the telephone rang and news of Andrew Jack's survival was made known to them. Dr Kennedy went over to the croft and attended to the gunner's injuries before an ambulance arrived to take him to the hospital at Lybster, north-east of Dunbeath.

It was stated by the President of the subsequent Court of Enquiry, Wing Commander Arthur W. Kay, that Dr Kennedy had been the first medical officer on the scene of six RAF crashes within two years, toiling over difficult terrain at the age of over seventy to attend to the victims. Confirmation came from Group Captain N.A.P. Pritchett, the officer commanding RAF Wick, who pointed out that two weeks earlier Dr Kennedy had climbed to within 200 feet of the top of Scaraben (1,900 feet) to attend to the men of a crashed Anson, and was largely responsible for saving two lives. It is now a pleasure to record that this indefatigable and gallant old gentleman was made a Member of the Royal Victorian Order by King George VI.

The body of the Duke of Kent was taken to Dunrobin Castle, the home of his friend the Duke of Sutherland. From there, it was borne to London and the funeral took place on Saturday 29 August at St George's Chapel in Windsor.

On Sunday 30 August, Andrew Jack's mother and sister were allowed to visit him in hospital, for the first time since the crash five days before. He was a distressing sight, sedated and propped up in bed, with his hands and face unbandaged but painted in gentian violet. He could barely speak through caked lips. While they were there, officers of the RAF's Court of Enquiry came into the room, and the two ladies were ushered outside. When they returned, Andrew had given a statement to the officers, one of whom held his hand so that he could sign it.

On 7 October 1942, Sir Archibald Sinclair, the Secretary of State for Air, rose in the House of Commons to make a statement about the findings of the Court of Enquiry. Getting the date of the crash wrong as 15 August instead of 25 August, he said:

> The court found: First, that the accident occurred because the aircraft was flown on a track other than that indicated on the flight plan given to the pilot, and at too low an altitude to clear the rising ground on the track; secondly, that the responsibility for this serious mistake in airmanship lies with the captain of the aircraft; thirdly, that the weather encountered should have presented no difficulties to an experienced pilot; fourthly, that the examination of the propellers showed that the engines were under power when the aircraft struck the ground; and fifthly, in accordance with King's Regulations and Air Council Instructions, paragraph 1325, that all the occupants of the aircraft were on duty at the time of the accident. The Chief Inspector of Accidents is in agreement with the findings of the court.

This statement was, of course, published in Hansard and reported in the press. Doubtless the authorities hoped that it would close a very unhappy incident, but for those experienced in wartime flying it raised as many questions as it settled.

Sir Arthur Conan Doyle put many sayings into the mouth of Sherlock Holmes, but the advice the great detective gave to Doctor Watson in *The Sign of Four*, published in 1899, might well be relevant to an investigation into the death of the Duke of Kent and the other occupants of Sunderland W4026: 'How often have I said to you that when you have eliminated the impossible, whatever remains, however improbable, must be the truth?'

Perhaps such an investigation should start with an examination as to whether there had been a 'cover-up'. This type of allegation crops up with tedious regularity every time I investigate an air mystery involving a public figure. It seems to me that the conspiracy theorists put forward their views because they are under the impression that they are difficult to deny and they know that the media will sensationalise the ideas or fantasies that have entered their minds.

In this instance the possibility arises since the file giving the detailed results of the Court of Enquiry into the accident is not available. The place where this could be lodged is the Public Record Office at Kew. Documents there fall into two broad categories: those released for public scrutiny after thirty years and those under 'long closure'. The results of RAF courts of enquiries generally come under a seventy-five year rule, but I happen to know that most of the wartime files, numbering several thousand, were weeded out by the Inspecting Officers many years ago and destroyed, apart from a few examples under Class AIR 2.

However, to find out whether the file on the enquiry in this instance had been preserved, I wrote to the Records Administration Officer and received a reply stating that it was not there. It was suggested that it might have been transferred to the Royal Archives at Windsor Castle, but a further letter brought a reply stating that it was not there and moreover had *never* been in their files. Thus it is evident that the file has been destroyed, together with almost all others. No. revelations will become available for researchers in the future. However, there are very important items of information from the Court of Enquiry which can be found elsewhere, as will be seen shortly.

Associated with the 'cover-up' theory is the known fact that Andrew Jack was at first very reluctant to discuss the crash, giving rise to the suspicion that he knew something that he was not allowed to disclose. However, such reluctance is very common among airmen who have been through terrible experiences, primarily because they try to blot them out of their minds. There is another factor which may have caused his initial reticence. According to *The Times* of London, which reported this crash very fully: ' . . . all the occupants had been killed. Some had been burnt; others had been thrown clear of the machine but had *died of their wounds*' [my italics]. This account is at variance with the report made by Dr Kennedy, now in the Public Record Office. However it is possible that Andrew Jack began his agonising journey in an attempt to help those of his comrades in whom he thought he saw flickers of life. At the time, he could have been reluctant to cause distress to relatives with this story.

Then Andrew Jack read in the newspapers that the blame for the accident was placed on a man whom he admired and respected, Frank Goyen. He knew that the officer on the flight deck with by far the greatest experience in Sunderlands was his captain, and the pronouncement in the House of Commons must have seemed grossly unfair to him. This apparently harsh verdict was in fact quite normal in such circumstances. If there was no mechanical fault in the aircraft and no extenuating circumstances such as extremely bad weather, then the fault always lay with the captain, according to RAF thinking and custom. Even if it could be ascertained that some other crew member had made an error, it was the responsibility of the captain to identify and correct it. Andrew Jack was incensed and bitter when he read the verdict. But I doubt if he really knew what had caused the crash. If he had known what went wrong, then the officers on the flight deck would also have known and the crash would not have happened.

As time went on, Andrew Jack began to express his feelings and beliefs to his family and friends. These consist of allegations that the Duke of Kent persuaded the crew to take off in bad weather, that he was at the controls when it crashed, and that drink was being consumed in the aircraft. His family have repeated these allegations to the national press, and some newspapers have given prominence to them.

The allegation that the Duke persuaded the crew to take off in bad weather is patently untrue. On the day of the crash the RAF's Chief of Air Staff, Air Chief Marshal Sir Charles Portal, wrote to Winston Churchill: 'Weather conditions over the first part of the journey were as follows: Cloud 1,000 ft; visibility 3 miles. There was, however, a bad patch off Wick where the clouds were at 300 ft. North of the north coast of Scotland, the weather improved; clouds were 4 to 8/10ths at 2,000 ft, and still further improvements would have been experienced further north and west.'

Any pilot of Coastal Command would have been perfectly happy to fly in such conditions and no persuasion from the Duke of Kent or anyone else would

Cheerful members of the ground crews of No. 228 Squadron, at Oban in June 1942. *(Tim Wilson collection)*

have been necessary. There should have been no danger at all if the crew had been able to keep to their instructions at briefing, which included flying at 2,000 feet and keeping clear of the east coast of Scotland.

Similarly, the story about the Duke being at the controls has no validity. I received a letter from Corporal Tim Wilson, who was a fitter in No. 228 Squadron at the time. His letter included the following: 'I was the Fitter II Engineer who was responsible for servicing, checking and refuelling the plane some days prior to it leaving Oban [No. 228 Squadron's base] and the flight to Invergordon.'

Corporal Wilson then described his friendship with the NCOs in the crew, including Sergeant Andy Jack, and his presence at Invergordon when they were briefed for the flight to Iceland by the aircraft captain, Flight Lieutenant Frank Goyen. His letter continued: 'Not until Andy Jack arrived at our base in Northern Ireland in the early part of 1942 [Lough Erne] did I have, other than Press reports, any information about the crash. . . . I met him in the maintenance hangar and we had a brief chat. He assured me that the boat was going fine, that the commanding officer, Wing Commander Moseley, was in number one seat, Flight Lieutenant Frank Goyen was in number two, and the Duke of Kent was standing between them.'

Andrew Jack must have seen those crew positions soon after take-off. It was his duty shortly after they were in the air to enter the rear turret, close the steel doors behind him, face backwards and turn the turret from side to side to keep watch for enemy intruders. He could not see the flight deck from the turret. The crew on the flight deck, including the navigator, could talk directly to each other but the rear gunner was connected only by intercom, and the rule was silence unless something vital needed to be said. Andrew Jack was still in the turret at the time of the crash.

Moreover, his description of the positions in the flight deck conforms with the finding of the Duke's body. He was not in the seat of either pilot but had been thrown clear of the wreckage, with his head completely crushed and his briefcase close behind him.

The allegation that alcohol was being drunk is even more serious. But according to information given to me by the Station Commander at Invergordon, Group Captain Geoffrey Francis, some of the *passengers* probably had a drink in the Officers' Mess before take-off, but there is no evidence that the officer members of the crew did so. It is possible that crates of drink were loaded on to the Sutherland, although there is no documentary evidence to support this. The Duke of Kent was flying to Iceland in his capacity of Inspector-General of RAF Welfare and such supplies would have been very welcome at the isolated stations he intended to visit. But anyone who flew in the RAF knows that the suggestion that the crew began drinking from such supplies is preposterous. There was, and still is, a rule that drinking alcohol before or during a flight was completely forbidden. Anyone who did so faced a court martial, but the matter was even more serious than this disgrace. It was an act of suicidal irresponsibility bordering on lunacy, and all aircrew knew this. The idea that Wing Commander Moseley or Flight Lieutenant Goyen would have permitted it is ridiculous.

In six years of wartime flying, I never heard of any such case. The allegation made by Andrew Jack and repeated to the press by members of his family enraged the men of the No. 228 Squadron Association. Their Secretary, Flight Lieutenant Eric N. Harrison, sent a letter to me which included the following: 'It is scurrilous and I am surprised that a quality newspaper like *The Sunday Times* [24 March 1996] should stoop to print something like that. . . . I did 700 hours of operations in Sunderlands with 228 Squadron and never, ever did I see alcohol on the plane. Have you ever heard of such rubbish? . . . We have 180 ex-members of 228 in our Squadron Association, at least 20 of whom were on the squadron at the time of the crash in 1942, and none of them believe the story about drinking.'

Quite apart from the nonsensical aspect of this allegation, there are the practical circumstances. The crew went out to the Sunderland about half an hour before take-off and during the brief period they were on board must have been fully occupied with their detailed pre-flight checks and duties. There was no time to start a drinking spree.

Andrew Simpson William Jack was born at Grangemouth on 8 May 1921. After a long period as an NCO in the RAF he was commissioned towards the end of the war, on 12 January 1945. He remained in the RAF until his retirement as a flight lieutenant on 6 June 1964 and thereafter worked as a telephone engineer. It seems that his accounts of the crash were at first quite rational but grew with the telling over the years. According to his RAF friends, he sometimes suffered from bouts of depression and began to drink heavily. It appears that he felt a sense of bitterness and needed to apportion blame for the accident. His death took place on 22 March 1978 at Brighton General Hospital from a combination of broncho-pneumonia, pancreatitis and cirrhosis of the liver, when he was only fifty-six years of age.

Another possibility which has been put forward is that the crew of the Sunderland deliberately deviated from their flight plan in order to carry out a sight-seeing tour of the east coast of Scotland for the benefit of their royal passenger, and then foolishly cut across the north-east corner of Scotland to reach Iceland without checking land heights. In particular, the home of the Duke and Duchess of Sutherland, Dunrobin Castle, was only ten miles to the west of their flight plan.

However, I do not believe that the men on the flight deck were so irresponsible that they would have taken this action, nor do I believe that the Duke of Kent would have abused his authority to ask them to do so. The flying boat carried depth charges. Dunrobin Castle had been partially converted into a military hospital and indeed the Duke's body was taken there after the crash, before burial in the grounds of Windsor Castle. There was a standing order from Coastal Command to the effect that flying boats were not permitted to fly over land except in an emergency, for the obvious reason that they could not land on the ground but needed fairly sheltered water on which to alight. Even on the short trip from Oban to Invergordon, the route would have been first northwards up Loch Linnhe as far as Fort William, then over the Caledonian Canal and associated lochs towards Moray Firth and Invergordon. If the weather had been unsuitable, the route on that flight would have been all the way up the west coast of Scotland to Cape Wrath, then along the north coast to John o'Groats and down the east coast to Cromarty Firth.

Moreover, there is positive evidence that the crew was not deliberately flying over land. Group Captain Francis instructed the crew to keep clear of the east coast of Scotland and to climb until they were well above the high ground before turning towards Iceland. In addition, it can be demonstrated that the Sunderland was descending when the crash occurred. If one draws a line on an ordnance survey map towards the site of the crash, either from the south or south-east, it becomes obvious that the Sunderland must have flown over ground several hundred feet higher before it crashed at Eagle's Rock. The obvious implication is that the pilot was deliberately descending, unaware that he was over cloud-covered hills.

This can be confirmed from three other sources. Perhaps the best account of this

Dunrobin Castle, at Golspie in Sutherland, viewed from the air. The Duke of Kent's body was taken there after the crash of the Sunderland on 25 August 1942. The castle had been partially converted into a military hospital at the time. *(Dunrobin Castle Ltd)*

The Duke of Kent's body was brought by train from Dunrobin Castle to Marylebone station in London on 28 August 1942. The coffin was draped with the Duke's personal standard and carried past a Guard of Honour to an RAF ambulance, as shown here. It was taken to the Albert Memorial Chapel at Windsor to await the funeral. *(Author's collection)*

tragedy was written many years ago by Ralph Barker, in his book *Great Mysteries of the Air*. In the early 1960s Ralph Barker was able to communicate with Andrew Jack, and it is probable that the two men were in sympathy with each other, for both were former wireless operator/air gunners who had survived serious crashes. Andrew Jack said that he could 'feel the sinking feeling as the aircraft descended'. The second source can be found in the memorandum written by the Chief of Air Staff, Sir Charles Portal, written to the Prime Minister, Winston Churchill, a few hours after the crash. This stated that the aircraft was headed for a position 'off Wick' but must have somehow drifted too far to the west. The third source is the Court of Enquiry itself. At the Air Historical Branch (RAF) of the MoD are summary cards for every RAF aircraft lost accidentally during the Second World War and on each are entered, briefly, the conclusions of any Court of Enquiry. In the case of Sunderland W4026 the entries are similar to those which appear in Hansard, but with one important addition. It states: 'Responsibility for serious error rests with captain of aircraft who changed flight plan for reasons unknown and *descended through cloud* [my italics] without making sure he was over water and crashed.'

Only one conclusion can be drawn from these facts. The crew on the flight deck believed that they were over the sea, not over the land. In the air, the captain of an aircraft was responsible for any decisions which varied from his briefing. There are two possible reasons why Goyen decided to descend rather than continue to climb. It is known that Prince George (as the Duke of Kent was entitled when King George V was alive) disliked flying in cloud when he served in the Fleet Air Arm in the interwar period and always asked to come out of it. If he was upset when the Sunderland was climbing through cloud, this may well have influenced the captain's decision. The other reason concerns navigation, which in Coastal Command depended largely on contact with the surface of the sea, enabling the navigator to take drifts on the white flecks below with the drift recorder situated alongside him in the Sunderland. These drifts gave the angles between the directions of the aircraft through the air and the tracks over the ground or the sea, caused by the wind. Using these in combination with the 'wind lanes' on the surface of the sea – long streaks which look like oily lines from above – the navigator could calculate the wind velocity and keep a continual 'dead-reckoning' position on his chart. This was not the only navigational technique used, but it was the primary one during daylight.

The Sunderland was a very stable aircraft to fly, with the ailerons and elevators needing only fingertip control and the rudder just a little more pressure. But it did suffer from one disadvantage – it was a very heavy aircraft at 58,000lb, with a wing loading of about 36lb per square foot. It climbed very slowly when fully laden, at only about 200 feet per minute, and it had a steep rate of descent. As a safety measure in case two engines should fail, the crews normally cruised at about 2,000 feet, but they would descend lower if necessary. The other flying boat in service at the time, the Catalina, had a wing loading of 24lb per square foot and often cruised lower, at about 500 feet.

Sunderland W4026 must have taken a run of about three miles before it became airborne. The recorded time of take-off, 1310 hours, is probably when it began this long run. It then climbed and returned to circle over its base, presumably as a farewell salute, turned again and flew via the entrance to Cromarty Firth and then from Tarbat Ness to Eagle's Rock, a total map distance of about fifty miles from Invergordon. If one takes into account the extra manoeuvres over Cromarty Firth, this reconciles fairly accurately with the total time it seems to have been in the air, only about half an hour. We cannot tell exactly when it entered the cloud, but this is likely to have been about ten minutes before the crash. It is probable that, with the deep hull of nearly thirty-three feet and visibility down to fifteen feet, the crew on the flight deck did not see the ground until a fraction of a second before the moment of impact.

The major question remains. What caused the flying boat to stray to the west of its intended track? To attempt to answer this, it is necessary to continue the process of elimination.

One of the suggestions put forward during the war was that the Sunderland was flying along a radio beam which the Germans contrived to bend and thus lure it to disaster. Bending radio beams was in fact a technique which British scientists achieved in late 1940 when the German *Knickebein* system of two intersecting radio beams, used for dropping bombs over British cities and towns, was identified and jammed, or 'bent'. But the RAF did not use such a system for long-range navigation. There was a short-range system, the Lorenz blind-approach, which consisted of the transmission to the aircraft's receiver of a series of dots on the left of its track and a series of dashes on its right; when the aircraft was directly on track to the signal, these dots and dashes merged into a continuous signal. However the Lorenz system, although similar in principle to *Knickebein*, could not be jammed in Scotland from Europe. In any event, it was not used on an outward journey such as the one on which the Sunderland was flying. Indeed, its use on the Sunderland III had been discontinued a few weeks before.

Another possibility which has been put forward suggests that the magnetic compasses in the Sunderland were affected by local magnetic disturbances caused by metallic rocks in the region. In his revised version of *Great Mysteries of the Air*, published in paperback by Javelin, Ralph Barker included a letter from a Spitfire pilot who flew over Berriedale in 1945 and estimated that his compass went out of true by as much as 50°. The pilot quoted the instance of a four-engined bomber which had crashed nearby shortly before and stated that the station navigation officer at Wick thought that there must be something in the region which caused this magnetic aberration.

By coincidence, I also flew over this coastline in 1942, as a squadron navigation officer in Coastal Command, and cannot remember any abnormality in the direction of compass needles; neither can any of my friends who flew in similar circumstances. However, having discussed the matter with Ralph Barker, I wrote to the British Geological Survey at Edinburgh to ask for an expert report. A very detailed reply provided the information that the magnetogram for the day of the crash, 25 August 1942, indicated that the magnetic field in the area was very quiet. But the reply also included the following:

'The area in which the Sunderland flying boat was operating has a high incidence of magnetic anomalies. A magnetic anomaly is a region on the earth's surface where the intensity of the magnetic field is concentrated either positively or negatively owing to the distribution of magnetic materials in the surface rocks. Their effect on navigation is difficult to predict . . . generally the strength of these anomalies is in the order of two or three per cent of the normal magnetic field of the earth.'

In order to find out the effect of this anomaly on the compass, I wrote to the Admiralty Compass Observatory at Ditton Park in Slough and received a reply from their RAF Liaison Officer, Flight Lieutenant Roger Small, who formerly navigated Shackletons and helicopters. His reply assured me that the anomaly would have had no significant effect on a magnetic compass, and included the following comment: 'In fact, for the first part of the journey up the coast of the Moray Firth, the aircraft would have flown *along* a magnetic anomaly contour and therefore experienced no effects from local disturbances at all.'

As a matter of interest, I then researched the circumstances of the four-engined bomber which crashed near Wick and found that it was a B-17 Fortress of an RAF meteorological squadron. The Court of Enquiry found that the pilot used defective radar readings (ASV) to home on Wick instead of requesting a wireless bearing, failed to take note of a diversion signal, failed to make a navigation check with Gee radar, failed to ask for the barometric pressure at base and had the wrong pressure set on his altimeter when he crashed. Unfortunately five of the nine men on board were killed. The accident was attributed not to magnetic anomaly but to pilot error resulting from fatigue after flying for ten hours.

The next matter to examine is one that will occur to every air navigator – the question of wind velocity. Could an unexpected increase in wind speed have pushed the Sunderland 15° west of its intended track? A visit to the Meteorological Archive at Bracknell and a scrutiny of the forecasted and actual winds for the place, date and time, revealed that there was an increase in speed from Beaufort force three to force four, a matter of five or six miles per hour. The direction was the same as forecast, from the east-south-east. If uncorrected on the aircraft's course, this would have caused an error of only two or three degrees west of the intended track. It accounts only partially for the error which actually occurred, about fifteen degrees west. To do this, the wind speed would have had to increase to Beaufort gale force ten, about fifty miles an hour, and this certainly did not happen.

In my opinion, this enquiry is left with an examination of two navigational instruments, both of which the commanding officer would have been anxious to demonstrate to the Duke of Kent. The first of these is the air to surface vessel radar, ASV Mark II. This device, which operated on 176 megacycles, comprised a directional transmitting and receiving system. The transmitter sent out a series of high-power pulses and the receiver picked up the resulting echoes from objects on the surface of the sea, displaying these on the screen of a cathode ray tube, which was situated in the wireless operator's position. These echoes were shown as blips on a central vertical line on the screen, the distances of the objects being indicated on a mileage scale along this line. Broadside aerials mounted on top of the hull gave the ability to scan both to port and starboard of the aircraft, while another set enabled the operator to switch to a forward homing signal. It was quite a simple system, but the operator needed a fair amount of practice before he became adept. Its use was confined to Coastal Command. Later developments, such as H2S which was used by Bomber Command, contained a trace which revolved around the screen and presented a fairly accurate representation of coastlines and built-up areas, as well as ships; but these later developments were not fitted in Sunderlands until the centimetric ASV Mark IV, similar to H2S, arrived in 1943.

Although ASV Mark II could be effective in showing up surface vessels and useful as a homing device (in the hands of a good operator), it was not otherwise a very reliable navigational instrument. The following is an account sent to me by the navigator of a crew in a Catalina:

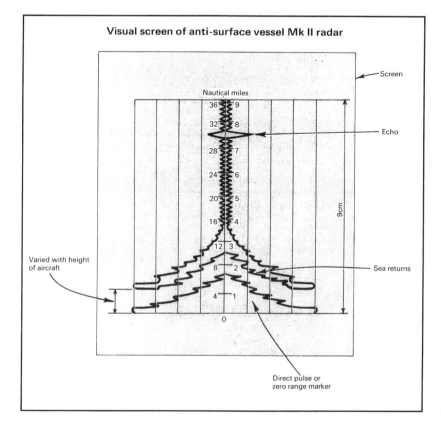

(Author's collection)

I can remember only once trying to 'navigate' by ASV Mark II and radar beacons, and the flight nearly ended in disaster. We were flying from Pembroke Dock in South Wales over the Irish Sea to Oban on the west coast of Scotland. There was 10/10th stratus cloud with heavy rain. We were flying at about 400 feet and visibility was nil. I tried to steer between Kintyre and the Irish coast by using the beacon on the Mull of Kintyre, keeping it on our starboard bow. We discovered afterwards that rain had soaked all the radar leads, causing a 40° squint. Consequently we passed to the *east* of the Mull of Kintyre instead of the west, and nearly hit the Isle of Arran. Fortunately, I regularly switched on to beam aerials and, discovering that there was land on both sides, we made a quick 180° turn to starboard. As we did so, our wingtip actually brushed some trees on Arran. We were carrying a new commanding officer at the time, and he was *not* impressed!

Could Sunderland W4026 have experienced a similar problem? It is possible but not highly likely. Certainly the crew would have wished to demonstrate the ASV to the Duke of Kent, for it was an instrument he may not have seen before in operation. There was a homing beacon at Wick, and the wireless operator may have demonstrated the rectangular blip which appeared on the screen, flashing the station letters in Morse and showing the distance away. But there was no rain. The only possibility is that moisture in the stratus cloud caused a squint, and that the pilot was asked to alter course to port to compensate for an apparently inaccurate heading, while flying in nil visibility. But the ASV Mark II had been in operation on No. 228 Squadron for about eighteen months and the wireless operators in the Sunderland were all highly experienced with the instrument. It is almost certain that the operator would also have switched on the beam aerials so that signals from the coastline would have shown up too. Moreover, the alteration of course would have been so large that it would have seemed wrong from a commonsense point of view. Goyen would not have reduced height if there had been any doubt about his position. He must have been confident that he was on a heading that continued over the sea.

We are now left with the operation of only one navigational instrument. This was the distant-reading gyro-magnetic compass (DR compass), which was a new device, installed in Sunderland IIIs only a few weeks before. It is possible that the members of the crew had had little, if any, practical experience with it.

The normal magnetic compass in the Sunderland III, as with many RAF aircraft, was the P4A, mounted horizontally by the first pilot's left knee. But this suffered from three disadvantages. Firstly, it was affected by acceleration and deceleration of the aircraft, as well as by centrifugal force, which could render it inaccurate during turns. Secondly, it was affected by magnetism from the engines and from metal in the pilots' cockpit. Thirdly, it was affected by the magnetic field of the earth itself, the difference between the true north and magnetic north, known as 'magnetic variation'.

The DR compass was designed to overcome these difficulties. The master unit was hung in a pod in the rear of the hull, where magnetism from the flying boat was negligible. Within this unit was a magnetic needle and a gyroscope, together with an electric motor. The needle prevented the gyroscope from precessing with the rotation of the earth, while the gyroscope gave stability to the needle, even during steep turns.

From the master unit in the Sunderland, an electrical transmission system transferred the compass heading to a repeater dial fitted in the pilots' instrument panel, where it replaced the 'beam approach indicator' dial. Other repeaters were installed by the navigator and by the bombsight. However, between these repeaters and the master unit was yet another device. This was the 'variation setting corrector', sited on the navigator's table. On this he set the changes in magnetic variation as the flight progressed. Over the north-east of Scotland in 1942 this was thirteen degrees west, as shown on the map.

We now come to what I believe is probably the heart of this problem. According to the navigator's manual at that time, Air Publication 1234, concerning the DR compass, 'the course he gives to the pilot need only be true'. In other words, the courses need not be adjusted for magnetic variation, since the variation setting corrector could take account of this. In my opinion, an error was made in one of three ways. The first possibility is that whoever was carrying out the navigation gave the pilot a true course to fly on the DR compass but did not adjust the variation setting corrector. The second possibility is that the pilot did not realise that the course he was given, perhaps over the intercom, was a true course intended to be flown on the DR compass, and clamped it on the P4A compass. The third possibility is that the settings on the compasses were correct when leaving Tarbat Ness but, if the variation setting corrector was being demonstrated to the VIPs, the knob was somehow twiddled back to zero.

The effect of each of these possibilities would have been the same: the aircraft would have flown thirteen degrees west of its intended track. Together with the slight increase in wind speed, this would have brought the Sunderland precisely over Eagle's Rock at the time the crash occurred.

We cannot be certain who was occupying the first pilot's seat at the time of the crash, except that it was not the Duke of Kent. According to the statement in the House of Commons, all crew members were at their places of duty when the Sunderland crashed. What is evident is that there was poor co-ordination on

The variation setting corrector on a distant-reading gyro-magnetic compass. *(Author's collection)*

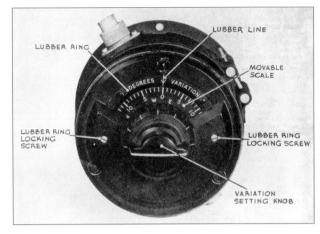

the flight deck. It has to be remembered that the officers had had very limited experience of flying together. Indeed, if the commanding officer is included, they had *never* flown together as captain, first pilot, second pilot and first navigator, apart from the short transit flight from Oban to Invergordon, which was probably accomplished mainly by map-reading. It is doubtful whether the vital element in a flying boat, teamwork, had had time to develop, in spite of the accumulated experience of some of the crew. Moreover, it is highly likely that the men were distracted, however unwittingly, by the presence of the VIPs. The section of the flight from Tarbat Ness to the site of

A navigator of a Sunderland checking the master unit of a distant-reading gyro-magnetic compass in a Sunderland. The instrument was suspended in the rear of the hull, where it was less affected by magnetic deviation from metal in the flight deck. *(Jeff Lloyd collection)*

The memorial on the site of the crash on 25 August 1942 of Sunderland III letter M serial W4026 of No. 228 Squadron, in which fourteen passengers and crew were killed, including the Duke of Kent. *(David J. Smith via Hugh J. Budgen)*

Part of the inscriptions on the plinth of the memorial, reading:

WING CDR.	T.I. MOSELEY	R.A.F.
FLT. LT.	F.M. GOYEN	R.A.F.
F.O	S.W. SMITH	R.A.A.F.
P/O	C.R. SAUNDERS	R.A.F.
FLT. SGT	E.J. HEWERDINE	R.A.F.
FLT. SGT	W.R. JONES	R.A.F.

(David J. Smith via Hugh J. Budgen)

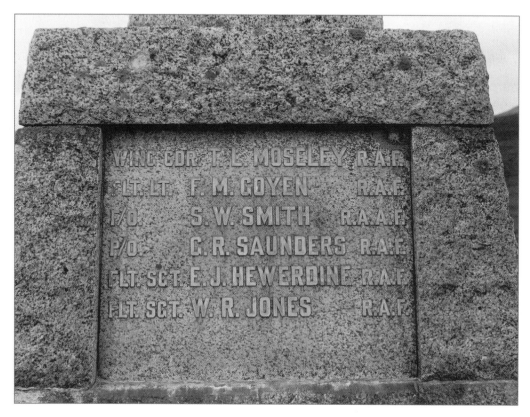

Above: Part of the inscriptions on the plinth of the memorial, reading:

FLT. SGT.	C.N. LEWIS	R.A.F.
SGT.	E.F. BLACKLOCK	R.N.Z.A.F.
SGT.	A.R. CATT	R.A.F.
SGT.	L.E. SWEET	R.A.F.
LT.	J.A. LOWTHER M.V.O.	R.N.V.R.
P/O	THE HON. M. STRUTT	R.C.A.F.
L.A.C.	J.W. HALES	R.A.F.

(David J. Smith via Hugh J. Budgen)

Below: Part of the inscriptions on the plinth of the memorial, reading:

IN MEMORY OF
AIR CDRE H.R.H. THE DUKE OF KENT
K.G., K.T., G.C.M.G., G.C.V.O.
AND HIS COMPANIONS
WHO LOST THEIR LIVES ON ACTIVE SERVICE
DURING A FLIGHT TO ICELAND ON A SPECIAL MISSION
THE 25th OF AUGUST 1942

MAY THEY REST IN PEACE

(David J. Smith via Hugh J. Budgen)

the crash would have lasted no more than thirteen minutes. That time may well have been occupied by demonstrating equipment to the VIPs instead of checking the settings on the compasses or verifying that the variation setting corrector had been properly adjusted.

In the earlier part of the flight from Tarbat Ness, the Sunderland was flying parallel with the coast. When the aircraft entered cloud, the curve towards the east of the coastline ahead might not have been visible to the pilots. After flying in cloud for several minutes, without any sign of clearance, the captain decided to reduce altitude to obtain sight of the sea so that normal navigation procedures could be resumed, unaware that they were approaching high ground.

The Court of Enquiry did not seem to analyse the cause of the navigation error, confining its remarks to 'captain changed flight plan for reasons unknown'. It is probable that they could not examine the settings on the navigational instruments, since the flying boat had burnt and melted. In any event, by comparison with enquiries into aircraft crashes these days, consisting of expert forensic examination of bodies and parts of the aircraft, RAF Courts of Enquiry during the war were fairly perfunctory affairs. There were thousands of them, occupying a great deal of time, and the business of prosecuting the war had to be given priority.

There is one matter which perhaps should be mentioned. In 1996 and 1997 I received several letters from Peter Rivers, a former RAF engineer, who has made a careful study of standing waves in the air, as used by glider pilots, and believes that these are underestimated by pilots in powered aircraft. He agrees that the Sunderland probably went off course from an error in the settings of the DR compass and diversion from their normal duties by the presence of the VIPs, but puts forward the view that the crew of the overloaded flying boat could have been forced to descend unwittingly by the 'strong sink which occurs on the down side of standing waves in the air'. It seems possible that this local phenomenon may have increased the rate of descent of the Sunderland beyond the norm and contributed to the crash.

This fateful flight ended in tragedy for the occupants of the Sunderland and their families. Some of the aircrew were nearing the end of their operational tours. Frank Goyen had had a particularly fine operational record up to this time and, if the circumstances had been only slightly different, he would probably have ended his tour with a decoration and possibly progressed to command his own flying boat squadron. I do not believe that the Court of Enquiry was correct in implying that he deliberately altered the flight plan. In my opinion, the crash was caused by a failure in communication, inexperience with a new navigational instrument, and very bad luck.

CHAPTER FIVE

Glenn Miller

The disappearance on 15 December 1944 of the famous band leader, Glenn Miller, has been followed by a mass of theories and counter-theories which continue to this day. One query which first arose in 1984 was passed to the Air Historical Branch (RAF) of the Ministry of Defence and treated with considerable scepticism. This is a small unit and the staff does not have the time to carry out investigations on behalf of the general public. Much of this research work involves the Public Record Office at Kew, where most of the wartime official documents are now held, as well as other places of research.

When a member of the MoD staff suggested that I carry out an independent investigation into this matter, I was intrigued at the prospect of trying to solve

Alan G. Ross, fan of Glenn Miller's music and researcher into the subject of his disappearance, in the Private Flying side of Liverpool Airport in September 2001. *(Alan Ross collection)*

a mystery which was then forty-two years old. I had no preconceived idea of what could have happened to Glenn Miller and indeed had only a very vague memory of his disappearance all those years ago. Nevertheless, I was familiar with the methods of research, was considered adept at finding my way through documents at the Public Record Office, and had gained a lot of knowledge of the problems of flying during my service in the RAF from 1939 to 1946.

The official file on the subject was made available to me and I was allowed to photocopy the contents. It included correspondence with Alan Ross, a member of the Glenn Miller Society, which proved very valuable to part of the research. However, this evidence did not clearly demonstrate that the death of Glenn Miller had any connection with the RAF, since he was a major in the USAAF and a passenger in a US military aircraft when he lost his life. But as my researches continued, I was able to uncover many new facts and relate these to his death. Nevertheless, it should be stressed that this is not an official explanation and that responsibility for the conclusions is mine alone.

Alton Glenn Miller was born on 1 March 1904 in the small town of Clarinda in Iowa. He was the second son of Lewis Elmer Miller and his wife Mattie Lou, with another boy and girl to follow. His father was kind and intelligent but never achieved commercial success. He worked as a carpenter, a janitor, a homesteader and a railway bridge foreman. The family moved from state to state and at one time lived in a rather primitive house in Nebraska. However, they were by no means unhappy. They were talented musicians and entertained themselves by playing a number of instruments in the evenings. Alton disliked his first name and insisted on being addressed as Glenn.

In 1923 Glenn Miller entered the University of Colorado, but withdrew after a while to play the trombone in a series of dance bands. He settled in the city of New York in 1928, arranging music for various bands. In March 1937 he made an unsuccessful attempt to form his own band, but was persuaded to try again a year later. By 1939 he had produced a distinctive form of music, based on the reed-section sound of a clarinet over saxophones, which soon became known as the 'Glenn Miller sound'. This met with a remarkable success and his band became by far the most famous in the USA. It made hit recordings, played in leading theatres and ballrooms, broadcast on the radio from coast to coast, and appeared in two Hollywood films. Glenn Miller became both a national and an international celebrity, and his recordings have endured to this day.

In the autumn of 1942, when at the peak of his career and popularity, Glenn Miller joined the US Army. He later transferred to the US Army Air Force, where he directed the Band of the Training Command. His laudable intention was to bring his music to the men in the front line and 'give them a taste of home'. Largely on the instigation of Colonel Edward M. Kirby, he and his band were sent to the UK for the benefit of US personnel in the European theatre. Glenn Miller flew to England on 18 June 1944, soon after D-Day and the invasion of Normandy. His band of sixty musicians and organisers included many with top-ranking talents who had been drafted into the US armed services. They arrived in the liner *Queen Elizabeth* at Gourock in Scotland on 28 June 1944, after a fast and safe passage across the North Atlantic. General Dwight Eisenhower had seen the need to provide a radio station, the AEPF, to broadcast entertainment and news to the invasion forces, and the Glenn Miller orchestra was destined to play an important part in this service.

Captain Glenn Miller of the USAAF. *(Ken Seavor collection)*

Glenn Miller was a hard taskmaster who began a punishing work schedule which took him and his band to many army and air force bases in the UK. Servicemen crowded into the concerts and received the music with rapturous enthusiasm. The band, which was eventually named the American Band of the Allied Expeditionary Force, broadcast regularly on BBC radio, as one of the 'big bands' which were the vogue of the day and still have their ardent followers. In appearance, Glenn Miller was tall and broad-shouldered, and he wore rimless spectacles which accentuated his rather studious and professional manner. His voice was easy and confident, introducing the rich and melodious numbers which typified the style and power of the strongest nation on earth.

The band was based at Bedford, where the men were safer from the V-1 flying

Major Glenn Miller conducting the American Band of the Allied Expeditionary Force in HMV's Abbey Road Studios in London on 16 September 1944. The band is probably playing *Farewell Blues*, the one instrumental number they recorded in this session. *(Ken Seavor collection)*

bombs which had begun to arrive over the British capital on 13 June 1944. Here they recorded their programmes for the BBC. However, Miller spent some of his time in a suite of rooms in the Mount Royal Hotel in London. His programmes came under Maurice Gorham of the BBC and were produced by Cecil Madden.

As the Allies advanced from Normandy, Glenn Miller promised the troops that he would give a live performance in Paris over Christmas. When the French capital was liberated on 23 August 1944, he became determined to make good his promise. During November he flew to Paris and was invited to return with his band in the following month, to entertain the forces over a six-week period. When they heard of this plan, both Gorham and Madden did their best to stop him from going. But Glenn Miller was adamant. In a marathon session of eighteen days, he and his band recorded a total of eighty-eight programmes, in addition to twenty-three regular broadcasts. The BBC could broacast these recordings in their absence.

Meanwhile Miller's manager, Lieutenant Don Haynes, flew to Paris to arrange accommodation and other matters, and then returned to Bedford. On 12 December 1944, General Dwight Eisenhower sent an order from his Supreme Headquarters of the Allied Expeditionary Force to Major Alton G. Miller, instructing him to proceed to the Continent by military aircraft 'on or about' 16 December 1944, with a baggage allowance of no more than 65lb, and to return to his present station on completion of his instructions. Miller immediately decided to go ahead of his band. He intended to fly in an aircraft of the US Air Transport Command from Air Station 112 at Bovingdon, near Watford in Hertfordshire. He waited in London for a suitable opportunity throughout 13 and 14 December, but the weather was too foggy for take-off. Haynes drove down to London on 14 December, picked up the band leader and returned to Bedford with him late in the same day.

A friend of the two men was Lieutenant Colonel Norman F. Baessell, from the nearby base of Milton Ernest, the headquarters of a US Service Command. Baessell frequently flew to Paris and offered to give Glenn Miller a lift on the following day, in a Noorduyn C-64A Norseman. This aircraft was on the strength of US Station 547 at Abbots Ripton in Huntingdonshire (now part of Cambridgeshire), the base for the 35th Depot Repair Squadron of the 2nd Strategic Air Depot Detachment, part of the US Eighth Air Force. This Service Command was commanded by Brigadier General Donald Goodrich. Abbots Ripton did not have its own airfield but there were facilities at the nearby US Air Station 102 at Alconbury, four miles north-west of Huntingdon. In December 1944, Alconbury was utilised by the US Eighth Air Force for training purposes and as a development unit for various radar devices, as well as serving as the flying field for Station 547 at Abbots Ripton.

The Norseman was a Canadian aircraft, built in Montreal. It was a single-engined high-wing monoplane, of a type which had been in service as a civilian utility aircraft before the war. The RCAF used it in wartime mainly as a trainer for wireless operators and navigators, but it also had a role in liaison and light transport. It was quite large for a single-engined aircraft, with a span of 51 ft 6 in and a length of 32 ft. The seating accommodated two in the pilot's compartment forward of the wings, while the cabin aft could take up to eight passengers or two tons of freight. The engine was almost the same as that fitted to the North American Harvard trainer, a Pratt & Whitney Wasp R-1340-AN-1 of 600 hp, radial, nine-cylinder and air-cooled, with a proven record for reliability.

This utility aircraft was not only employed as a wheeled landplane but could also be adapted to take with floats or skis. It was particularly suitable for the rugged terrain and extreme climatic conditions of the vast area of Canada. The USAAF had ordered a number of this aircraft. It employed some in Arctic bases but others were stationed in East Anglia for liaison work. The RAF had only a few, and these were stationed in Canada as part of the Empire Air Training Scheme.

The pilot of the Norseman allocated to carry Glenn Miller and Norman Baessell to Paris was Flight Officer John S.R. 'Nipper' Morgan, a US citizen who had been born on 14 June 1922 at Hamilton in Scotland, the son of a coal miner. The family had emigrated to the USA and made their home in Detroit. Morgan had volunteered for the RCAF in 1942 and trained in Canada and then England, before transferring to the USAAF on 23 May 1943, with under 500 hours in his pilot's log book. His rank in the USAAF was equivalent to a Warrant Officer in the RAF and he was engaged on light liaison or ferrying work. According to one of his fellow pilots, he was competent at visual flying but not proficient at instrument flying or pilot-navigation. He had had no combat flying experience, either in the RCAF or the USAAF.

The Norseman flown by Flight Officer Morgan had been allocated the US serial number 44-70285 (1944 being the year of manufacture) and it probably carried the 470285 part of this number. According to the crew chief, it was painted in the standard olive drab over medium grey, and of course it bore the normal USAAF markings. The ultimate destination was Bordeaux, but a stop was to be made at US Air Station A-42 at Villacoublay, about ten miles south-west of the centre of Paris. This was an advance air depot for the Service Command of the US Ninth Air Force, which was engaged on tactical support for the Allied land forces in Europe. The Norseman's journey was classified as a type A mission, or a non-operational flight.

Boeing B-17G Flying Fortress serial 43-37599 letter O, named *Moonlight Serenade*, with two members of the ground crew standing under the two 0.50 inch machine-guns in the chin turret. The photograph was taken at Knettishall in Suffolk on 26 August 1944, the day after Glenn Miller and his Band of the Allied Expeditionary Force gave a concert for the 388th Bombardment Group of the US Eighth Air Force at this station. This Fortress did not return from a mission on 5 September 1944, when the 1st Bombardment Division despatched 303 Fortresses against oil installations at Ludwigshafen in south-west Germany. It was on the strength of the 562nd Bombardment Squadron and flown by 2nd Lieutenant Raymond Paaske. *(Richard T. Tosaw collection)*

Morgan was ordered to pick up Miller and Baessell at RAF Twinwood Farm, an airfield four miles north of the centre of Bedford. First opened in 1941, this was a satellite of RAF Cranfield, about eight miles south-west of Bedford, which in turn was part of RAF Fighter Command's No. 12 Group. Twinwood Farm was used primarily for training the crews of Beaufighter night-fighters of No. 51 Operational Training Unit.

The early morning of Wednesday 15 December was foggy and overcast throughout much of south-west England and the Midlands. The wind was very light indeed, coming from the south-east at no more than 5 mph. It was cold, with a temperature of about freezing point at ground level. Baessell telephoned

Lieutenant Don Haynes of the USAAF, who was Glenn Miller's executive officer, right-hand man and close personal friend. He drove Glenn Miller and Norman Baessell to RAF Twinwood Farm on the morning of 15 December 1944 and was the last person to speak to them before they took off in the Noorduyn Norseman and disappeared. *(Richard T. Tosaw collection)*

Miller at Bedford to say that the weather should be clearer later in the morning and that it would be possible to take off. Haynes drover Miller in a staff car to Milton Ernest, to have an early lunch with Baessell, and then took the two men the few miles to Twinwood Farm to await the arrival of the Norseman.

The flying control clerk on duty in the control tower at Twinwood Farm was Leading Aircraftwoman (LACW) Anne Carroll, who was experienced in this type of work. She had already served as a plotter with Fighter Command's No. 13 Group headquarters at Ouston, Newcastle upon Tyne, and then worked in the operations room of Bomber Command's No. 3 Group at Exning, near Newmarket in Suffolk. Her memories of 15 December 1944 are sharp and clear. Flying training had been cancelled, owing to the fog, so that the normal busy work schedule did not exist. However,

A Noorduyen C-64 Norseman of the USAAF in flight. The Canadian company produced 749 during the Second World War, the majority being purchased by the USAAF. *(Author's collection)*

Flight Officer John R.S. Morgan of the USAAF, the pilot who took off in the Norseman from RAF Twinwood Farm on 15 December 1944, with Lieutenant-Colonel Norman Baessell and Major A. Glenn Miller as passengers. He was known as 'Nipper' or 'Pee Wee' by other pilots in his unit, but as 'Johnny' by aircraftwomen of the WAAF at Twinwood Farm. *(Ken Seavor collection)*

Lieutenant Colonel Norman Baessell of the USAAF, who offered Glenn Miller a lift in the Norseman from RAF Twinwood Farm to Paris on 15 December 1944. *(Ken Seavor collection)*

Anne Carroll, the Leading Aircraftwoman who served as a flying control clerk at RAF Twinwood Farm and signed off the Norseman carrying Glenn Miller to Paris on 15 December 1944. The photograph was taken post-war when she was employed by British Overseas Airways Corporation. *(Anne Carroll)*

Three Leading Aircraftwomen of the Women's Auxiliary Air Force (WAAF) who were at Twinwood Farm when the Norseman carrying Glenn Miller took off at 1355 hours on 15 December 1944. Left to right: Zelda Marks, Anne Carroll, Thelma Callow. On the far right is Doug le Vicki (now deceased) of the Glenn Miller Society. The photograph was taken on 28 August 1994 in front of the control tower at Twinwood Farm. *(Alan Ross collection)* the control tower always remained open, day and night, with the Flying Control Officers and their clerks working in shifts. A telephone call came through from US Station 547 at Abbots Ripton to inform them that a Norseman of the USAAF would land and then fly on to US Air Station A-42 at Villacoublay. Next came a call from the guard room of their station to say that a US Army car was at the main gate and required permission to drive to the control tower. The authority was duly given.

With little else to occupy her time, Anne Carroll was able to look down from the control tower and see the car draw up on the hardstanding and the three US officers get out. They stood there with the collars of their raincoats turned up and with their hands in their pockets, obviously waiting for the aircraft. She recognised Glenn Miller immediately, for he had flown from the station before, usually in a Cessna Crane twin-engined monoplane piloted by a Captain Carnell of the USAAF, and had also given a concert on the station. But she did not know the other two officers.

According to Lieutenant Don Haynes, he and the other two men wondered if the pilot would be able to locate Twinwood Farm through the low cloud, but after a while the Norseman duly appeared. The standard procedure was for the pilot to request permission to land over the R/T to the Flying Control Officer on duty, who was also a pilot. The airfield had three runways. Morgan landed on one of these and then taxied round the perimeter track to the front of the control tower. He did not get out and Anne Carroll watched as Glenn Miller and the other officers walked towards the Norseman. Don Haynes stated that at first Miller was reluctant to enter it, for he disliked flying and asked why there were no parachutes. Apparently Baessell laughed and made one of his ribald remarks: 'Do you want to live forever?'* Miller and Baessell got into the Norseman, the door was closed and Morgan taxied back round the perimeter track before taking off. Anne Carroll noted the time in the log book in the flying control. It was 1355 hours local time. The Norseman disappeared and not a single message was heard from it again.

On the following Saturday, LACW Anne Carroll was off duty and about to leave the camp when a message came over the Tannoy loudspeaker, instructing her to report immediately to the control tower. She had already dressed in civilian clothes under her service greatcoat but rapidly changed back into her uniform

---

* Attributed to Frederick the Great at the Battle of Kolin on 18 June 1757. When his Guards hesitated in a charge, he shouted: 'You dogs, do you want to live forever?'

and arrived in haste. Two tall Americans were waiting to question her, introduced by the Flying Control Officer as from the FBI. They were wearing civilian clothes, one in a navy blue suit with brown shoes and the other in a rather loud sports jacket and slacks. She was told that the Norseman had failed to arrive at Villacoublay, and replied to their queries about the landing, take-off and destination. They took notes and left the station.

The band was scheduled to fly to Paris on the following day, in C-47 Skytrain Dakotas of the US Air Transport Command. They were sent down to Bovingdon but once again the weather proved too foggy and they returned to Bedford. Finally, three C-47 Skytrain Dakotas of the 315th Troop Carrier Command, US Ninth Air Force, flew on 18 December to Twinwood Farm from US Air Station 493 at Spanhoe in Northamptonshire. They picked up the band and their instruments and flew to US Air Station A-47 at Orly, near Paris, which was one of the bases in France for the US Ninth Air Force. The men were surprised to find that Glenn Miller was not there to meet them or direct their activities. According to Don Haynes, he began enquiries by telephoning Supreme Headquarters Allied Expeditionary Force (SHAEF) at Versailles, but was told that they had no information. He then telephoned Brigadier General Goodrich and learnt that the Norseman had not landed at Villacoublay and was missing.

Whenever a famous – or infamous – person disappears, rumours and theories abound. In the case of Glenn Miller, these were prolific at the time and they continue to this day. He had defected to the enemy. He had survived, horribly mutilated, and was living in seclusion. He was not on the Norseman but had left the aircraft at Bovingdon. He had been found with a crushed skull at Place Pigalle, one of the red light districts of Paris, having been associated in some way with the black market in France. He had died of lung cancer in a British military hospital, his death concealed by the British who, for some unknown reason, wished to insinuate that he had been shot down by an enemy fighter. There are always authors who pander to the public appetite for 'conspiracy theories' by concocting such stories as well as publishers willing to produce their books, irrespective of any private views of their authenticity.

To some extent, these conspiracy theories have been fuelled by the fact that the USAAF did not announce Glenn Miller's disappearance until Christmas Eve. Meanwhile the recordings made before his flight continued to be broadcast, the listeners unaware that the famous band leader had lost his life. However, such a delay in a public announcement was quite normal with all US or RAF servicemen who disappeared on a flight for unknown reasons. The procedure was, at first, to make enquiries as to whether the aircraft had landed at some intermediate point.* If these enquiries proved negative, the following procedure was to notify the next-of-kin, usually by telegram. These gave condolences but usually required the person not to transmit any information to the press. The purpose of such secrecy was to defer any announcement which could be of use to the enemy. Irrespective of the circumstances, it was a normal requirement. The press was usually given the names of missing personnel after about ten days or a fortnight.

Of course, it may be argued that Major Glenn Miller was such an important person that the normal rules should have been waived. But even if the US authorities had contemplated such an action, they had other and more vital matters to occupy their minds. The day after the Norseman disappeared, the Wehrmacht attacked through the Ardennes with the intention of cutting a wedge through the Allied armies as far as the Belgian border and wiping out the surrounded men in the northern sector. It even seemed for several days that they might succeed, as the Battle of the Bulge raged. The efforts of the Western Allies were devoted to this great struggle.

It is certain that Brigadier General Goodrich would have been informed immediately of the missing Norseman but any who knew of the loss would have observed the usual secrecy until the next-of-kin had been informed and the news was generally released.

The 'Missing Aircrew Report', prepared by the headquarters of the USAAF in Washington on 23 December 1944, states that the Norseman took off at 1355 hours on 15 December 1944 and that nothing was heard from it after that time.

The occupants were:
> *PILOT*   MORGAN, JOHN R.S., F/O; MISSING
> *PASSENGER*   BAESSELL, NORMAN F., LT COL; MISSING
> *PASSENGER*   MILLER, ALTON G., MAJOR; MISSING

I find it impossible to believe that the US authorities would have falsified this information, with the complicity of high-ranking officers and the RAF control tower at Twinwood Farm. Without wishing to detract from Glenn Miller's achievements, I do not think he would have been considered so important at the time as to require a 'cover-up' to conceal the circumstances of his death. In the British newspapers, his fate did not warrant more than a few lines, while some ignored it entirely.

---

* This happened to me in 1942, when flying from the south coast of England to Scotland. We landed with engine trouble at an intermediate RAF airfield but for some reason a signal was not sent to our destination. Eventually our crew was traced and our next-of-kin were not notified.

In this analysis, the time of take-off is very important. It would have been written in the log book as local time, although this record no longer exists. All the records of the US Eighth Air Force were also written in local time, as were those of the US Ninth Air Force in Britain and north-west Europe. During the war, local time in Britain was one hour ahead of the time we have at present. From 0200 hours on 2 April 1944 to 0200 hours on 17 September 1944 we had British Double Summer Time (BDST), two hours ahead of Greenwich Mean Time (GMT). It then changed to British Summer Time (BST), one hour ahead of GMT; this rather incongruous name for the winter months was sometimes referred to as 'British Single Time'. Thus the local time of 1355 hours for the take-off from RAF Twinwood Farm was one hour ahead of GMT.

Apparently Morgan did not leave a flight plan and told no one of the route he intended to follow to Villacoublay in France. At first sight, this seems to present an insuperable problem to a researcher. However, if one examines the navigational circumstances of the time, it is possible to determine the route, for it must have been influenced by the defences against V-1 flying bombs.

The arrival of these German weapons had been anticipated by the British and many preparations were made. Defences were set up along the south-east coast of England and funnelled in towards London. More balloons were brought to the south-east of London and between these and the coast a greater number of anti-aircraft guns and fighter squadrons were deployed. The guns and crews were American as well as British, for General Eisenhower declared that London was an American as well as a British base. The code name for the V-1 flying bomb was 'Diver'.

At first, there was a great deal of confusion between the gunners and the pilots, for the anti-aircraft fire sometimes hit a pursuing fighter. Something had to be done to separate these means of defence. On 15 July 1944, Air Defence of Great Britain circulated a change of plan. The anti-aircraft guns in front of the balloon barrage were to be removed forthwith and placed along a coastal strip known as the 'Diver Gun Belt'. This extended from a position five miles east of Beachy Head in Sussex almost as far as Dover in Kent. Between this Diver Gun Belt and the balloons around London, the fighters were free to tackle the flying bombs. In the words of the directive, 'complete freedom of action against flying bombs will be allowed to AA guns at all times and in all conditions within the boundaries of the new Diver Gun Belt'. Aircraft were permitted to fly over this belt if above 10,000 feet, but it can be imagined that the USAAF and the RAF avoided it like the plague.

Of course, the events of the war did not remain static and by August 1944 the Allies had overrun most of the launching sites of the flying bombs in northern France. The Germans responded by launching some of them from Heinkel Hellls over the North Sea. From 8 September, they also began sending the more deadly V-2 rockets against London, from sites in the Netherlands and northern Germany. Thus most of the guns in the south-east belt were moved to the east coast as well as a new 'Diver Gun Box' to the east of London. The great balloon barrage to the south-east of London was also shifted to a more easterly position. Nevertheless, pilots usually preferred to avoid the old gun belt as well as these new areas.

As a liaison pilot, Morgan must have known of these prohibited areas. His route must have bypassed them, and he would have avoided the war zone over the North Sea as well as the German enclave of Dunkirk, which had been invested by the Allies on 7 September and did not surrender until the end of the war. The only logical route he could have followed was firstly to US Air Station 112 at Bovingdon, on a southerly course. From there, it would have been the correct procedure to continue southwards to the easily recognisable landmark of the Thames, thus avoiding the prohibited area of Greater London. From the Thames, he would have been able to set course direct for Villacoublay, crossing the south coast of England near Newhaven and the French coast near Dieppe. This is the most direct route he could have taken and moreover was the one used regularly by the US transport aircraft from Bovingdon when flying to Paris. It was known as the 'SHAEF Shuttle'. It would have brought the Norseman into Villacoublay well before sunset, which was at 1648 hours BST in Paris on that day. The USAAF did not normally fly at night, if it could be avoided.

However, the identification of the route does not in itself establish the fate of the Norseman. The view has been put forward that it might have crashed in the fog and been lost in thick woods somewhere in England. The likelihood of this is very remote indeed. It is true that wartime aircraft are still being recovered in Europe, from lochs, lakes, fjords, polders, remote mountains and boggy ground. But the route over England does not contain such features. It is fairly densely populated and had no serious navigational hazards at the time. Some remains of the aircraft would have been discovered long since. It is infinitely more likely that the Norseman went down somewhere in the English Channel.

For a long time it has been thought that icing may have been the cause of the disappearance. Certainly icing was a problem with piston-engined aircraft during the war. One form was known as 'airframe icing', which could affect the wings, fuselage or tail. This happened when rain fell on an aircraft and immediately froze, spreading back from the leading edges of the wings. It could vary from a light semi-crystalline coating, which was not very dangerous, to a heavy glazed frost which could seriously affect the aerodynamic characteristics of the aircraft. However, glazed icing seldom occurred in England, being more common over North America and Scandinavia. Experiments showed that it could form when the cloud temperature was in the range of minus 1 to minus 10 degrees centigrade. It occurred in cumulus clouds or, far more seriously, in the cumulo-nimbus clouds which pilots always avoided unless they flew into them inadvertently. However, although the Norseman was not equipped with wing de-icers, it could not have been brought down by airframe icing. The records in the National Meteorological Archive at Bracknell in Berkshire show that neither the temperature range nor the clouds were present over the Channel on that day. In contrast to the foggy conditions in the early morning over part of the area to the north-east of London, the weather on the south coast was quite clear at 1400 hours BST, with a visibility of about 15 miles and a ground temperature of about plus 8 degrees centigrade.

The other form of icing was 'engine icing'. There were three types. The first was caused by impact ice at the entrance to the air intake, somewhat similar to airframe ice; but this depended on rain, which did not occur over the Channel on this day. The second was throttle ice, formed when the relative humidity of the air was 100 per cent and the temperature was less than 3 degrees centigrade; again, these conditions did not exist. The third form was more deadly. It was called carburettor icing, and could form when petrol mixed with air, owing to the latent heat of evaporation. Experiments showed that the range of conditions was far greater than either impact or throttle icing: up to 10 degrees centigrade, with the relative humidity 50 to 100 per cent. These conditions were certainly present over the Channel on that day, as they were on many other days of the year. However, it is known that the carburettor of the Norseman was fitted with a heating device, and was thus unlikely to have iced up unless there was some malfunction.

My original guess was that icing was the most probable cause of the loss of the Norseman, but after examining the synoptic charts and other records of the weather conditions it seemed one of the least likely. I also found that many other aircraft flew over the Channel at the same time as the Norseman and none experienced any icing.

One aspect of the episode puzzled me. If Morgan had experienced icing, or maybe engine failure, it is reasonable to expect that he would have sent a distress call. A Mayday call was an extremely high priority for any pilot going down in the sea. The Norseman was fitted with the transmitter/receiver SCR-274-N, often called a 'coffee-grinder' by the US airmen, giving a voice-to-voice contact of at least 100 miles. But nothing was heard from Morgan. It is possible that the set was not functioning, set to the wrong frequency, or modified for shorter range, but it seems far more likely that he did not have time to use it. It is also possible that he was forced to ditch with engine trouble which was unconnected with icing. But the sea was smooth, the wind light and the visibility extremely good over the Channel. One would expect the pilot and the passengers to have managed to inflate the dinghy and get into it.

The end of the Norseman appears to have been sudden and violent. I therefore turned to the matter which the Air Historical Branch particularly wanted me to examine, the possibility of an RAF involvement in the affair. This produced some very unexpected results. In order to relate them, it is necessary to change the scenario to an RAF bomber base.

Victor Gregory volunteered for the RAFVR towards the end of 1940, at the age of nineteen. Born in Wolverhampton, he was a railwayman, as was his father. He applied for aircrew training as a wireless operator/air gunner, but was soon told that he had the qualities necessary for pilot training. After remustering as a pilot, he began training at No. 16 Elementary Flying Training School at Burnaston, near Derby. His course was short-lived, however, for he was soon posted to the USA under the Arnold Scheme. This plan, devised by General Henry H. 'Hap' Arnold, allocated a number of places for RAF trainees in US flying training schools, before the USA entered the war.

Gregory was one of the first RAF trainees to enter this scheme. He began on Stearman PT-17 biplanes at Lakeland Field in Florida. Then he moved to Cochran Field, near Macon in Georgia, where he flew in the Vultee BT-13A Valiant monoplane. His final training in the USA took place at Moody Field in Georgia, firstly on the single-engined North American AT-6 Texan and then on the twin-engined Cessna AT-17 and the Curtiss AT-9 Jeep I.

With the rank of sergeant, Gregory returned to the UK. His performance had been rated as 'very good' and there was a shortage of instructors. After taking a flying instructor's course, he was posted to No. 14 Elementary Flying Training School at Elsdon (now the airport for Birmingham), where he taught pupil pilots how to fly Tiger Moths. Then his commission came through and he was sent as an instructor to his old station of Burnaston.

Gregory continued as a flying instructor until March 1944, when he took a conversion course on the Airspeed Oxford at No. 18 Advanced Flying Unit at Snitterfield, near Stratford-on-Avon, as a prelude to becoming a bomber pilot. Then he was posted to No. 85 Operational Training Unit at Husbands Bosworth, near Leicester, where he converted on to the Vickers Wellington. Here he formed his crew, all save the flight engineer. His navigator was Pilot Officer Fred Shaw, who had trained in Canada. Pilot Officer Ivor Pritchard was the bomb aimer, Sergeant Bob O'Hanlon the wireless operator, Sergeant Eric Arnold the mid-upper gunner and Sergeant Harry Fellows the rear gunner. The crew was destined for an operational squadron on Avro Lancaster heavy bombers.

The men then moved to No. 1653 Heavy Conversion Unit at Chedburgh, near Bury St Edmunds, where they were joined by their flight engineer, Sergeant Deryck Thurman. Here they trained on four-engined Short Stirlings. Then the crew was sent to No. 3 Lancaster Finishing School at Feltwell in Norfolk. Finally they were posted to Methwold in Norfolk, the base for No. 149 Squadron of Bomber Command's No. 3 Group.

By the time he and his crew arrived on this operational squadron, Victor Gregory was a very experienced pilot by wartime standards, with 1,350 hours in his log book. He was happy with his crew, who were all young but steady, as well as competent and cheerful. They were ready for the gruelling strain of an operational tour in Bomber Command. This consisted of thirty operational flights from which, according to postwar statistics, less than 30 per cent survived during 1943 and 1944.

It was now December 1944 and the end of the war in Europe was almost in sight. For the past four years, Bomber Command had flown over Germany and occupied Europe almost entirely at night. Its equivalent on strategic bombing, the US Eighth Air Force, had flown for over two years on daylight attacks, thus providing 'round the clock' bombing. The American heavy bombers, B-17 Fortresses and B-24 Liberators, were escorted by long-range fighters. In March 1944, the Americans had begun to gain ascendancy over the Luftwaffe's Bf109s and Fw190s with the advent of the remarkable P-51B Mustang. This fighter, with an American airframe and a Rolls-Royce engine, out-performed all other piston-engined fighters. Fitted with drop-tanks, it could escort bombers to any target in Germany during daylight.

By then, the Allies dominated the skies over western Europe. Thus Bomber Command had begun to resume some daylight attacks, escorted by Mustangs in addition to the shorter-range Spitfires, while continuing its powerful night bombing. The first of these daylight operations had taken place in June 1944 with attacks against V-1 flying bomb sites in northern France. They had been extended eastwards as the Allies advanced towards the German border until, by late September 1944, cities in western Germany felt the weight of Bomber Command's great bombs in daylight.

The first operational flight for which Victor Gregory and his crew were detailed was a daylight attack on the German town of Siegen, about fifty miles east of Cologne. The date was 15 December 1944. It was to be a sizeable attack, consisting of 138 Lancasters of No. 3 Group, escorted by over 100 Mustangs of Fighter Command. Apart from No. 149 Squadron, the bomber force included

Nos 15 and 622 Squadrons from Mildenhall, Nos 90 and 196 Squadrons from Tuddenham, No. 75 (New Zealand) Squadron from Mepal, No. 115 Squadron from Wratten Common, No. 514 Squadron from Waterbeach and No. 218 Squadron from Chedburgh. All these bases were fairly close to each other.

The bombers were ordered to take off and form up en route to Bury St Edmunds in Suffolk and then Bishops Stortford in Essex. The fighters were all based in East Anglia and ordered to take off at a later time and eventually link up with the bombers. The Lancasters were to fly in close formation, in vics of three or boxes of four. The tactics were similar to those of the US Eighth Air Force, except that the American bombers usually formed up in diamonds of eight. But the British bombers carried over twice the bombload of the American aircraft.

The route of the bomber formation continued towards Gravesend on the south bank of the Thames, after passing through the narrow corridor between the balloon barrage to the east of London and the Diver Gun Box. The next turning point was Beachy Head on the south coast, slightly to the west of the

The crew of Lancaster I letter K serial NF973 of No. 149 Squadron, photographed after 15 December 1944 in front of another Lancaster. Left to right: Sergeant Eric T. Arnold (mid-upper gunner); Sergeant Deryck Thurman (flight engineer); Flying Officer Ivor J. Pritchard (bomb-aimer); Flying Officer Victor H. Gregory (captain and pilot); Pilot Officer Fred H. Shaw (navigator); Sergeant Robert H. O'Hanlon (wireless operator); Sergeant Harold Fellows (rear gunner). *(Flight Lieutenant Victor H. Gregory DFC)*

Lancaster I letter B serial HK795 of No. 149 Squadron at Methwold in Suffolk. This is the Lancaster in which Flying Officer Gregory and his crew completed their operational tour. The normal letters of No. 149 Squadron were OJ, but the letters TK were painted on several aircraft in preparation for the expansion of one of the flights into a new squadron, which was never formed. *(Flight Lieutenant Victor H. Gregory DFC)*

south-east Gun Belt. From here, the route was over the Channel to a point near Amiens in France, then turning east towards Siegen. This would have taken them over territory which for the most part had already been occupied by the Allies and was thus free of enemy flak. They were to fly as low as possible on the way out, to keep below the German radar, but then climb to 16,000–18,000 feet for the final bombing run.

The time of the attack on Siegen was originally scheduled for 1400 hours GMT, but the crews were delayed for about an hour before take-off, since there was uncertainty about the weather over the fighter bases. These were further east, and the morning fog was proving slower to clear in that direction. Victor Gregory and his crew were keyed up, anxious to acquit themselves well on their first operational sortie. They had not yet been allocated their own Lancaster and had to borrow one normally flown by another crew, letter 'K for King' serial NF973. While they were waiting, a member of that crew came over to the flight engineer, Deryck Thurman, and told him in unrepeatable terms to bring it back in one piece.

Gregory finally took off at 1137 hours GMT. In discussions with me, he said he could remember that a New Zealander, Pilot Officer L.F. Robinson, was the captain of one of the Lancasters in his vic, but he could not remember the captain of the other aircraft. The weather was still a little misty but there was clear sky above the ground layer.

All went well at first, although forming up took some time before the bomber stream was able to set course. They continued on their allotted route, but then each wireless operator in turn received a recall signal. The Mustang pilots of Fighter Command were unable to take off after all. According to one of their squadron records, they could not see the end of their runway. However, another reason may have been that the squadrons had only recently converted from Spitfires to Mustangs and the pilots were less familiar with their new aircraft.

The Lancasters could not return immediately to their bases, for their loads were too heavy for landing. All were carrying a 4,000lb blast bomb known as a 'cookie' or a 'blockbuster'. In addition, each carried 8,000lb of other bombs. Most of these consisted of 4lb incendiaries in 500lb containers, but in a few of the leading aircraft these containers had been replaced with 250lb target indicators. Although this was a daylight raid, Bomber Command still continued the tactics it employed at night. The target indicators were coloured red and green on this day, providing marker signals for the main bomber stream behind the leading aircraft.

The cookie was thin-walled, cylindrical in shape. It was fitted with a tail to stabilise its downward path and a domed nose in which were set three pistols

A 4,000lb blockbuster bomb being loaded on a Lancaster preparatory to take-off from a snow-covered airfield. Lancasters frequently carried this cylindrical bomb, which was sometimes called a cookie since it was often dropped when incendiaries tumbled out of large canisters carried by the same aircraft. The lateral blasts of the bombs combined with fires from the small incendiaries were considered the most effective method of laying waste to built-up areas. *(Author's collection)*

Ten Lancasters forming up to join the main bomber stream on a daylight raid. *(Author's collection)*

and exploders. The pistols were arranged at different angles to ensure that at least one struck the ground. There were two more exploders in the rear end. This bomb, which had a very high charge/weight ratio to provide a maximum blast effect, incorporated an unusual design in the exploders. In the rather mild words of the notes issued to US bomb disposal personnel in 1945: 'It has been reported that the diaphragm has been reversed by the cushion of air built up by the bomb as it neared the ground.' This meant that the firing pin fired just above the ground, giving an enormous lateral blast. The purpose of this was to knock down as many buildings as possible while the incendiaries set fire to the ruins and continued the work of destruction. Moreover, it was impossible to drop the bomb unfused or 'safe', since the nose crushed on impact. In fact, the cookie was a highly sensitive bomb. All pilots in heavy bombers were under orders *never* to try to land with one of them and always to drop the bomb from at least 3,500 feet, to avoid being caught in the enormous blast.

There were three areas designated for jettisoning bombs. One was in the North Sea off the Wash, another off the Thames Estuary, and the third was the Southern Jettison Area in the English Channel. No. 218 Squadron, which had despatched twelve Lancasters, was the first to be recalled and headed for the North Sea. The others flew to the Southern Jettison Area. The centre point of the latter was 50.15N 00.15E, and it was considered dangerous to fly within a ten-mile radius of this point.

The times of recall varied considerably among the Lancaster squadrons. Some received their recalls while still over England, some while over the Channel and some while over France. Victor Gregory and the remainder of No. 149 Squadron had passed Amiens and reached the 'south of Brussels' leg before they turned back.

Each captain made his own decision about how many bombs to drop in addition to his cookie. The Operations Record Books of the squadron, now in the Public Record Office at Kew, vary greatly in the amount of detail recorded, dependent on the Squadron Adjutant and the Squadron Intelligence Officer concerned. However, it seems that about half the incendiaries were dropped, as well as all the cookies.

In Gregory's Lancaster, Ivor Pritchard selected the entire bomb load. He looked through his Mark 14 bombsight at the sea below, to check whether there were any aircraft beneath them or whether any ships had strayed into the prohibited area. The Lancasters were flying at heights between 4,500 and 7,500 feet, and Gregory was at the lower level. Pritchard dropped the bombs. 'They're going off', he said over the intercom.

In the Lancaster, the navigator sat behind the chart desk, concealed by a blackout curtain. Here he marked the progress of the aircraft on his Mercator chart, referred to the screen of the Gee radar to plot its position and kept his navigator's log. But Fred Shaw was curious about the effect of the exploding cookies, which he had never seen before, and came out of his compartment to the position of the flight engineer, where there was a small blister window set in the starboard side of the fuselage. He could not see their own bombs, which had trailed behind them out of sight, but he could see shimmering grey blast waves radiating outwards from exploding cookies dropped by other Lancasters. The noises of the explosions were drowned by the roar of the Lancaster's engines.

'There's a kite down there', Pritchard said suddenly, from his position in the nose. 'Kite' was RAF slang for any aircraft, particularly one which could not be identified. Shaw continued to look until the strange aircraft came into his field of vision. It was a high-wing monoplane in camouflage colours, flying at about 1,500 feet towards them, in almost the opposite direction. Shaw recognised it immediately as a Norseman. He had trained in Canada, where the Norseman was used as a navigation trainer.

As Shaw watched, the Norseman dipped its port wing and, just before it would have disappeared from sight underneath the starboard wing of the Lancaster, dived into the sea. From the rear turret, Harry Fellows called out, 'There's a kite gone in. Did you see it?' Shaw replied, 'I saw it.' The term 'gone in' is significant. In RAF jargon it meant that the aircraft had dived uncontrollably into the sea. If the pilot had made a smooth belly landing, Fellows would probably have said, 'A kite has ditched in the sea.'

Glenn Miller's Last Flight
by Mark Postlethwaite GAvA

Victor Gregory's memory of this incident is somewhat hazy. He can remember that something significant happened on that day over the Southern Jettison Area, a conversation among his crew which caused him to look down at the sea, but he cannot remember exactly what it was. In any case, he was not in a position from where he could see the Norseman and thus has no visual memory. He flew on many operational sorties and after so many years those which were very eventful are more prominent in his memory. This does not surprise me. I now find that some events on a crowded period of operational flying have gone from my memory. Nowadays, my gunner can remember some important incidents such as an exchange of gunfire with a night-fighter, which I ought to remember but do not, probably because I was concentrating on recording our position. Similarly, I can remember clearly certain incidents which seemed to me dramatic from my position in the nose of a Beaufort but which my gunner has forgotten.

It is probably the visual aspect of such incidents which causes them to stick in the memory. Victor Gregory can certainly remember concentrating intensely on his flying, watching out for other Lancasters to avoid collision, and wanting to get home. The Norseman was not within the field of vision of Eric Arnold in the mid-upper turret. Deryck Thurman was busy making calculations and watching the instrument dials. Bob O'Hanlon was listening intently through his earphones for any wireless transmissions from base, especially since there was a possibility that the weather might close in again.

Fred Shaw thought that the Norseman was brought down by blast from the cookies and he may well have been correct. According to AP1661B Armament, issued to armament personnel, the safety height for dropping the cookie was 'at least 1,500 feet'. But this was a gross underestimate. By coincidence, one of the Lancasters of No. 149 on that day, serial NG362, had direct experience of the blast from a cookie. Flying Officer Harry H. Jones lost an engine immediately after take-off from Methwold and turned to the jettison area off the Wash, over the North Sea. His bomb aimer, Flying Officer James H. Woodward, has sent me a diary he kept and I also received a letter from his navigator, Sergeant Fred A. Biggs. The men were nervous at the prospect of heading towards Germany in daylight but reached the area and dropped the incendiaries from about 3,000 feet, although two clusters (each of thirty incendiaries) hung up within the containers. They continued gaining height and finally dropped the cookie 'safe' at about 4,000 feet. It exploded and even at this level blew the Lancaster about 1,200 feet upwards. Finally, they had the uncomfortable experience of landing with the two clusters of incendiaries threatening to break through the bomb bay and set the aircraft on fire.

In my view, however, the Norseman is equally likely to have been brought down by incendiaries. These 4lb bombs were made of magnesium alloy. They were 21.4 inches long and hexagonal in cross-section, being packed like honeycombs into small bomb containers, each containing 90 of them. The container remained on the aircraft and the incendiaries jostled each other as they fell out. Air pressure built up among them as they fell, spreading them in all directions. Over 100,000 incendiaries fell over the Southern Jettison Area on that day, from a long stream of Lancasters heading north.

Incendiaries were known to create a very considerable danger for bombers over enemy targets in Europe. As the official historians, Sir Charles Webster and Dr Noble Frankland, wrote in their history *The Strategic Air Offensive Against Germany 1939–45*:

> Owing to their light weight and enormous quantity they, therefore, spread over wide areas which not only made it impossible to concentrate them on or around the aiming point, but also created a hazard to the bomber stream. Bomber Command aircraft must, in fact, have been brought down by four-pound British incendiary bombs, and most crews with sustained experience of major operations endured at one time or another the unpleasant prospect of seeing their aircraft peppered with these dangerous missiles.

The incendiary bomb was not fully aerodynamic and soon reached its terminal velocity of 420 feet per second, or 286 mph. Nevertheless, this velocity was known to be enough for the bomb to punch through two storeys of a house before it began burning. The Norseman was built with a rather unusual mixture of Canadian spruce and steel struts, covered with fabric. A shower of incendiaries would have gone right through all parts of the aircraft other than the engine. They could have destroyed the control surfaces of ailerons or elevators, perhaps severing the control wires. One can imagine the pilot struggling to keep the aircraft in the air before it went out of control and dived into the sea. The bombs might even have killed the pilot or the passengers.

Victor Gregory flew on to Beachy Head and then continued between London and the Diver Gun Box. He landed at Methwold at 1420 hours, according to the Operations Record Book. On landing, there was no debriefing in the operations room, for this did not count as an operational flight. Instead, the crews were told to disperse to their rooms in the officers' and sergeants' messes, and to be ready for another attempt on the following day. Gregory and his crew were very tired, annoyed and disappointed. They had undergone much of the strain and effort of an operational flight, and it had come to nothing.

There is no mention of the sighting of the Norseman in any of the Operations Record Books of the squadrons involved, or in the records of Methwold. When a raid was aborted and there was no debriefing, such records were confined to times of take-off and landing, serial numbers of aircraft, bomb loads and names of crews, although in this case some records do mention the positions where the bombs were dropped within the Southern Jettison Area. However, Victor Gregory is certain that three members of his crew saw the Norseman plunge into the sea and that the matter was discussed briefly in the squadron.

It may seem extraordinary that no alert was sounded and no search was made for the occupants of the Norseman. However, this is to misunderstand the circumstances of operational flying in the Second World War. Firstly, the aircraft *dived* into the sea and there was no possibility of survivors. If by remote chance anyone had managed to get clear and did not drown, he would have died quickly of hypothermia in the wintry sea. Next, so many aircraft were lost in those days that this was just one among many, and moreover one which had flown unwisely into a prohibited area. Dozens of Allied aircraft could be lost in a single day and searches for the crews were not initiated unless there were positive sightings of survivors in dinghies. The air-sea rescue services did some extremely useful work but their resources did not stretch very far. Lastly, Victor Gregory believes that if anyone had tried to report the matter formally to their commanding officer, he would have been told not to waste his time. Such an attitude may seem callous today, but those who flew in the war had to become hardened to the continual flow of casualties. I can remember trying to report an aircraft burning on Lundy Island on one occasion, four Germans being washed from their dinghy and drowned on another, and a parachute floating in the water on yet another, but these failed to arouse any interest on the part of the intelligence officer.

There is nothing in the Operational Record Books of the air-sea rescue squadrons or the air-sea rescue marine units to indicate that a hunt was made for the missing Norseman. The only distress call on 15 December 1944 came from an aircraft over the North Sea. It is possible that some of these units may have been alerted to look out for wreckage of a Norseman after this day, but only when on other duties or patrols.

In spite of some foggy conditions on 15 December 1944, it was a day of intense air activity. Bomber Command sent 17 other heavy bombers to attack a target in Holland. The US Eighth Air Force (Bomber Command's partner in strategic bombing) despatched 674 heavy bombers and 434 fighter escorts from bases in East Anglia in daylight to attack German targets, losing three aircraft. Coastal Command despatched 82 home-based aircraft, including photo-reconnaissance, and one crashed on return. On the tactical side, SHAEF controlled the US Ninth Air Force and the RAF's Second Tactical Air Force from bases in south-east England and north-west France. These two tactical air forces despatched 1,199 bombers and fighters in support of the ground forces, losing seven aircraft. In addition, they sent out 82 aircraft on reconnaissance flights and 101 more on supply-dropping operations. Thus, 2,746 Allied aircraft in total were in the air on daylight missions. Moreover, these were followed immediately on night raids by 363 aircraft of Bomber Command on targets in Germany, with the loss of two of this number. The impression of the weather conditions created by the film *The Glenn Miller Story*, that of dense fog blanketing England, is quite erroneous. The fog was only patchy and general flying conditions were good.

No. 3 Group then despatched 108 Lancasters to Siegen in daylight on the following day, after the aborted raid of the day before. On this occasion, they were escorted by P-51 Mustangs of the US Ninth Air Force based in north-west France. One bomber was lost but many public buildings were destroyed and 314 people were killed. The business of war went on and the Lancaster crew had far more important matters to think about than the sighting of a crashing Norseman.

The question of timing should now be examined. According to the records, the Norseman took off from Twinwood Farm at 1355 hours and the Lancaster landed at 1420 hours. Thus at first sight it seems to have been impossible for the two aircraft to have met over the Channel. But there is a matter which is not immediately apparent. Navigators in the RAF did not record their times in their logs in BST or BDST. Most were issued with a special 'astro' watch, which was always set to GMT, and they ensured that this was accurate to the second. This was used in conjunction with official air almanacs and tables which were always recorded in GMT. The 'apparent' movements of the sun, moon, planets and stars could not be changed to conform with local times devised by governments. Navigators' flying logs written in the air were kept in GMT.

Of course, the fact that these navigators' logs were kept in GMT does not necessarily mean that the Operations Record Books written by Squadron Adjutants were also written in GMT. Indeed, the instructions contained in the present-day AP 3040 'Notes on the compilation of the Operations Record Book' specify that the records should be kept in local time. But the AP 3040 issued in wartime did not contain this stipulation. Where I have been able to check this matter with other enquiries, the times in Operations Record Books have always tallied with navigators' logs written in the air, when the squadrons were based in the UK. The same is true of No. 149 Squadron. I have been able to check one of Fred Shaw's logs, kept in GMT, with that of the Operations Record Book, and they are the same. The times in the log kept on 15 December 1944 by Sergeant Fred Biggs of No. 149 Squadron, which is still in his possession, also tally with the Operations Record Book.

Thus the landing of Lancaster NF973 at Methwold on 15 December 1944, recorded as 1420 hours, was in fact 1520 hours BST. We have seen earlier that the time of take-off of the Norseman was recorded as 1355 hours BST. It is now possible to plot the tracks of the two aircraft. The Lancaster experienced no delay in landing at Methwold, according to Victor Gregory's clear recollection. Its indicated airspeed, without bombs, was probably about 210 mph, giving a true airspeed of about 225 mph at 5,000 feet. With a light load, the Norseman probably flew at an indicated airspeed of 155

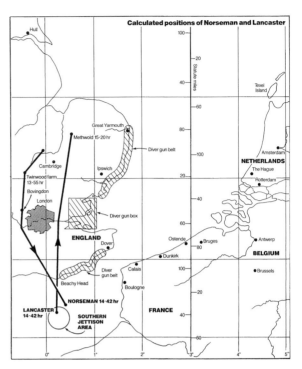

Calculated positions of Norseman and Lancaster.

mph, or 158 mph at 1,500 feet. The wind was from the south-east, probably 5 mph at 1,500 feet and 15 mph at 5,000 feet. If these facts (admittedly containing certain assumptions) are plotted on a chart, they show that the paths of the two aircraft would have been about 10 miles apart, close to the Southern Jettison Area. But if the Norseman was slightly off track, or made its turn further south than the Thames, it could easily have strayed into the prohibited zone at precisely the same time as the Lancaster.

Victor Gregory and his crew continued their operational tour. After about eight sorties, a ventral gun was fitted in their Lancaster and Flight Sergeant Frank Appleby joined the crew as an additional air gunner. Some of the events in their tour are still vivid in Victor Gregory's memory, far more so than the episode over the Southern Jettison Area. He can still hear Harry Fellow's words in his ears when they were attacked by a night-fighter over Bonn: 'Corkscrew port – go!' Their Lancaster was hit by flak many times, including the starboard fuel tank over Koblenz and the port engine over Ludwigshafen. On another occasion, an 88 mm shell went through an elevator and failed to explode. Over Gelsenkirchen, splinters of flak slightly wounded Deryck Thurman's face and missed Victory Gregory's throat by a whisker. One of the most terrible sights they saw was a Lancaster hit by a bomb dropped from above; it disintegrated and brought down another Lancaster. The crew completed a tour of 31 operational sorties and dispersed. Victor Gregory was awarded a DFC while Frank Appleby, who was on his second tour, received a DFM.

When the news of Glenn Miller's loss was announced on Christmas Eve, Fred Shaw put two and two together, but he did not know that the famous band leader was in a Norseman. The matter went into the back of his mind in the stress of his operational flying. He was demobilised after the war but in December 1951 rejoined the RAF and became a flying controller. In 1956, he saw the film *The Glenn Miller Story*, learnt that a Norseman was the aircraft involved, and was reminded of the incident over the Southern Jettison Area. He wrote to the *Daily Express* but received a reply stating that the matter was 'no longer newsworthy'. He accepted that this was the case. After nine years, ill-health forced him into premature retirement from the RAF. He emigrated to South Africa and became a consultant for mining equipment in the Witwatersrand gold mines. In 1984, he related his story about the Norseman to an all-ranks meeting of South African ex-servicemen known as the MOTHS (Memorable Order of Tin Hats). To his amazement, it caused a sensation. It was picked up by Henry Holloway, a South African broadcaster and promoter who is

Fred Shaw in the garden of his home in Johannesburg in November 1986. He died in October 1992. *(The late Flight Lieutenant F.H. Shaw)*

Henry Holloway (right), the South African broadcaster and promoter of popular music who interviewed Fred Shaw in 1984 and brought his story to the notice of the world. The photograph was taken in October 1999 in Los Angeles with Artie Shaw, the famous clarinettist and band leader who was a contemporary of Glenn Miller and an exponent of 'swing music' in the 1940s. *(Henry Holloway)*

a great fan of Glenn Miller's music. He interviewed and video-ed Fred Shaw on 29 April 1984 and the results were spread throughout much of the English-speaking world.

In turn, Alan Ross of the Glenn Miller Society in England began to research the matter assiduously and to raise queries with the Air Historical Branch (RAF) of the Ministry of Defence. He managed to find out what had happened to all the members of the Lancaster crew. Victor Gregory had retired from British Rail, as it was then called. For seven years before this retirement, one of his responsibilities had been to travel as officer-in-charge of the Royal Train for the Western Region. Bob O'Hanlon had retired as Deputy Chief Constable in the Staffordshire Police. Eric Arnold still ran his family business, while Deryck Thurman worked for the Central Electricity Generating Board. But none of these men saw the Norseman, or could remember much about the episode over the Southern Jettison Area forty years before.

Ivor Pritchard, the bomb aimer who first spotted the Norseman, had died. He never spoke to anyone about his RAF experiences. Harry Fellows, the rear gunner who saw the Norseman dive into the sea, had also died, but he had sometimes discussed his RAF experiences with his brother Maurice and his cousin Harry Penny. Both confirmed, most emphatically, that he had seen 'a kite go in' over the Channel on that day. Moreover, he told his brother that he believed the aircraft contained Glenn Miller.

Alan Ross wrote a summary of his researches and this proved very useful to my own enquiries. Eventually, my own conclusions corresponded very closely with his, after I had researched public and other records in great detail. But Alan Ross's conclusions were rejected by some at the time, for two main reasons. The first was that the routes of the two aircraft had not been established, nor the position of the Southern Jettison Area, and the times of the two aircraft did not seem to coincide. The other concerned the reliability of Fred Shaw's flying log book, for it was evident that the entries were in two different handwritings and the sceptics thought it might have been tampered with. The fact is, however,

Year 1944		AIRCRAFT		Pilot, or 1st Pilot	2nd Pilot, Pupil or Passenger	DUTY (Including Results and Remarks)
Month	Date	Type	No.			
—	—	—	'O'		—	— Totals Brought Forward
DEC. 14		LANCASTER I NF.970		F/O. WHITEN		AIR TEST.
				SELF.	CREW.	
DEC.	15	LANCASTER I	K NF.973	SELF.	F/O. SHAW. F/O. PRITCHARD. SGT. THURMAN. SGT. O'HANLON. SGT. ARNOLD. SGT. FELLOWS.	OPS.- SIEGEN. RECALLED. BOMBS DROPPED IN S'THN JETTISON AREA. 1×4000. 12×500. (INCENDIARY)
DEC.	17	LANCASTER I	E HK.652	SELF.	CREW.	BULLSEYE - LONDON - TOO MUCH CLOUD FOR PHOTOGRAPH.
DEC.	18	LANCASTER I	D HK.645	SELF.	CREW.	G.H. PHOTOGRAPHY - ELY CATHEDRAL. 12 PHOTOS. 316×
DEC.	19	LANCASTER I	L NG.355	SELF.	F/O. SHAW. F/O. PRITCHARD. SGT. THURMAN. SGT. O'HANLON. SGT. ARNOLD. SGT. FELLOWS.	OPS.-TRIER. DIVERTED TO MANSTON, FOG AT BASE. CONGRATULATIONS FROM GEN. EISENHOWER. FLAK HOLE IN STARBOARD ELEVATOR. NO FIGHTERS. (FIDO AT MANSTON) (1×4000. 4×1000. 4×250)

149 SQDN. METHWOLD.

GRAND TOTAL [Cols. (1) to (10)]

An extract from the Pilot's Log Book of Victor H. Gregory, written in his own hand.

12·44	1500	N.F. 970 LANCASTER F/o GREGORY	NAVIGATOR.	AIR TEST	1·15	
15·12·44	1200	N.F. 973 LANCASTER F/o GREGORY	NAVIGATOR	OPS. SIEGEN. CANCELLED. JETTISON SOUTHERN AREA	2·45	
17·12·44	1900	H.K.652 LANCASTER F/o GREGORY	NAVIGATOR	BULLSEYE LONDON.		3·15
18·12·44	1500	H.K 645 LANCASTER F/o GREGORY	NAVIGATOR,	G.H., ELY, AV. ERROR 316 YDS.	1·40	
19·12·44	1130	N.G. 355 LANCASTER F/o GREGORY	NAVIGATOR	OPS. TRIER, LANDED MANSTON ELEVATORS HOLED, LANDED FIDO.	4·50	
23·12·44	1130	N.G. 355 LANCASTER F/o GREGORY	NAVIGATOR	MANSTON – BASE	0·35	
24·12·44	1700	LANCASTER F/o GREGORY	NAVIGATOR	OPS. BONNE-HANGELAR AIRFIELD (FIGHTER ATTACK OVER ▲)		5·25
28·12·44	1400	HK 652. LANCASTER F/o GREGORY	NAVIGATOR	G.H. FRIDAY BRIDGE GH_U/S	1·05	
29·12·44	1530	H.K.699 LANCASTER F/o GREGORY	NAVIGATOR	OPS. KOBLENTZ. FLAK HITS LANDED MANSTON (TANK HOLED)	4·55	
31·12·44	1430	H.K.699 LANCASTER F/o GREGORY	NAVIGATOR	MANSTON – BASE	0·35	
				TOTAL TIME....	142·30	79·25

An extract from the Flying Log Book of Fred H. Shaw, written in his own handwriting apart from the totals at the bottom of the columns.

that some of the entries were written by Fred Shaw and others by Victor Gregory, who had the habit of bringing his crew's flying log books up to date from time to time, before submitting them to his flight commander for signature. In any event, the fact that Fred Shaw flew on that flight of 15 December 1944 can easily be substantiated at the Public Record Office.

An interesting comment on these events came from an unexpected source. On 15 December 1944, Beryl Seal was a WAAF nurse working at Station Sick Quarters at Mildenhall, the station from which Nos 15 and 622 Squadrons flew on the aborted raid. This young lady, who was a qualified nurse before the war, had also been trained by the RAF. Among her duties was nursing wounded airmen back to health, or attending to them when they were dying. Another was equipping the Lancasters with the contents of their first-aid haversacks. Thus she got to know some of the aircrews quite well, and later became the corporal secretary to the Station Medical Officer at the headquarters of No. 3 Group at Exning. In correspondence with me, Mrs Beryl Seal-Morgan stated that the story of the downing of Glenn Miller's aircraft was quite widespread among aircrews at the time, although they thought it was secret information.

Beryl Seal of the Women's Auxiliary Air Force, photographed in November 1942. *(Mrs Beryl Seal-Morgan)*

The Queen shaking hands with Victor Gregory, with the Duke of Edinburgh looking on. The photograph was taken in the evening of 2 November 1975 at Slough railway station, when the royal train was about to leave for Scotland. On this occasion, Victor Gregory travelled as Officer-in-Charge as far as Glasgow. *(Flight Lieutenant Victor H. Gregory DFC)*

Several Lancasters landed at Mildenhall at roughly the same time as Victor Gregory landed at Methwold.

Another letter came from a navigator of No. 622 Squadron, Gordon C. Dalton, who was acting as a bomb aimer in one of the Lancasters on the aborted raid. He remembered seeing the blast rings of the cookies exploding over the Southern Jettison Area. Although he did not see the Norseman, he watched a small fishing vessel leaving a long wake as it put on full speed to get out of the danger area. It is possible that this vessel was French and that the men were not aware that they were in a prohibited zone.

I also received an interesting letter from Sol Belinky in the USA, an ex-glider pilot of the 78th Squadron of the 435th Troop Carrier Group, US Ninth Air Force. He had participated in the D-Day landings, the invasion of southern France and the landings at Arnhem. On one occasion, he and a group of pilots were asked to ferry some light liaison aircraft, either Aeronca L-3s or Taylorcraft L-2s, from Liverpool to France. The date was about a week after the liberation of Paris. They landed on a small airfield on the south coast of England. This appears to have been RAF Friston near Beachy Head, which was also the base for two non-flying units of the US Ninth Air Force. After staying overnight, they lined up behind a Supermarine Walrus amphibian of the RAF, normally used for air-sea rescue, which began to shepherd them over the Channel in the direction of Dieppe. The cloud ceiling came down and Sol Belinky found that he was flying alone, without the guide. Then he was surrounded by spouts of water and realised he was in a jettison zone. Fortunately he was not harmed and landed somewhere near Dieppe, where he asked a farmer the way to Paris and eventually reached this successfully.

When I first began this enquiry, it was in a mood of scepticism about the story emanating from South Africa. Of course, the integrity of such a responsible and honourable person as Fred Shaw was beyond question, but I wondered if time might have played a trick with his memory. As I collected more and more information, however, I realised that the coincidences confirming his story were truly remarkable. I was also impressed with a comment in one of his letters to me: 'But, one thing is certain. You may struggle with times as much as you like but *I saw a Norseman go into the drink*. With my head in the blister on the starboard side I was watching the cookies detonating as they neared the surface of the sea and was fascinated by the sight of the shimmering, outwardly radiating, grey blast waves from them. It was then that I saw the Norseman.'

In another letter to me, he asked: 'If it wasn't Glenn Miller, then who was it?' The official RAF records confirm that no other high-wing monoplane was lost over the English Channel or in that theatre of war on 15 December 1944. In addition, the US official records at Maxwell Air Force Base in Alabama confirm that only one Norseman, No. 44-70285 in which Glenn Miller was a passenger, was lost on that day.

I was equally impressed by the statement made to me by Victor Gregory DFC:

My long period of service in the RAFVR was so crowded with incidents that it is difficult to remember the precise details of all that happened. My recollections of that aborted raid on 15 December 1944 are, firstly, waiting for the fog to clear sufficiently before take-off. Then I remember seeing the blast rings of the cookies exploding ahead of me over the Southern Jettison Area. Then there was a remark made by a member of the crew which caused me to look down into the sea, followed by a conversation among the other crew members. Although I cannot remember what the conversation was, I now believe it began with my bomb aimer drawing my attention to the approach of a light aircraft and ended with the sighting of it diving into the sea. But I was not in a position to see the aircraft and, as you know, it is visual experiences that one remembers best. I can say, however, that there was definitely some sort of incident over the Southern Jettison Area.

When this matter was first researched by Alan Ross of the Glenn Miller Society, I had a telephone call from Fred Shaw in South Africa. It was our first contact after leaving 149 Squadron and, after the excitement died down, I asked him if he was positive about seeing the Norseman dive into the sea. He replied, 'Vic, I definitely saw that Norseman go in. There is no doubt about that whatsoever.' Fred Shaw was not only an excellent navigator, but a most meticulous and precise person. He was, and still is, a man of complete integrity, and he has no wish for personal publicity in this matter. I am sure that his recollections are correct.

I was lucky to have a first-class crew in 149 Squadron and among these was the rear gunner, Harry Fellows, who has since died. His brother Maurice, who came to see me, assures me that Harry saw a light aircraft dive into the sea on the day, and I also believe that to be correct.

In a letter sent to Alan Ross on 14 April 1986, Maurice Fellows said:

I dearly wish that my brother Harry could be alive to confirm the evidence himself – he would have been so thrilled. However, I can confirm that he did mention it to me on more than one occasion.

The first time I was aware of the fact was some time in the 1950s when I went to see the film *The Glenn Miller Story*. I went to the cinema in the afternoon and was so taken up with the music that I saw the film through twice. I came home and spoke about the film to my brother, and it was then that he told me he believed that he had seen the Glenn Miller aircraft when returning from a bomber mission. He had witnessed a light aircraft going into the sea, along with other members of the crew, and some time later had married up the incident with the Glenn Miller disaster.

I am quite sure that my brother would never have invented such a story.

These comments, together with my own researches and calculations, were enough to convince me that the story was accurate and correct. Nevertheless, the final proof that Glenn Miller died because his pilot flew inadvertently into a prohibited zone could only come from the discovery of the remains of the Norseman at the bottom of the sea. The best estimate is that it crashed in the north-east quadrant of the Southern Jettison Area, which had its centre point about thirty miles south of Beachy Head. The cross-Channel ferry from Newhaven to Dieppe passes close to this area. It is covered by Admiralty charts on a scale of 1:150,000, number 2451 to the north and number 2612 to the south, with number 5011 giving an explanation of the symbols.

This position is also in one of the shipping lanes of the extremely busy English Channel. Although diving is permitted in the areas of inshore traffic (so long as the rules are observed), special permission has to be obtained in the one-way shipping lanes. Diving could be difficult and expensive, with over 100 vessels passing through each lane every day. Some years ago, I obtained an opinion from an expert in hydrography:

The area in which Glenn Miller is believed to have come down is in fact on the French side of the Channel, hydrographically speaking . . . it is extremely unlikely that it would be possible – more than forty years on – to detect, let alone positively identify, the small amount of wreckage involved. If it was made up of timber and fabric, this would have rotted, and the only substantial metal components, such as the engine, would long since have sunk into the sea bed, which consists of sand and gravel which is in itself mobile, both vertically and horizontally.

As you may imagine, the eastern English Channel has one of the most cluttered seabeds in the world . . . in my opinion, the chances of finding and positively identifying anything that might remain from Glenn Miller's aircraft are many millions to one against.

Thus there seems no chance of locating the wreckage of the Norseman. But there is one aspect of this matter which may occur to ex-airmen of the Second World War. Glenn Miller was not only an exceptionally talented band leader whose works continue to give pleasure to millions. He was also Major Alton G. Miller of the USAAF. Although his duties were non-combatant, he was subject to the hazards of war. Like many thousands of fellow-Americans, he died in the service of his country and the free world.

In August 1989 my earlier article on this subject was read by an American living in California, Richard Tosaw. He was a qualified lawyer who had been a special agent with the FBI for five years and had then formed the company Bureau of Missing Heirs. He had already investigated one of America's well-known air mysteries, the so-called 'D.B. Cooper' who had hijacked a Boeing 727 of Northwest Airlines on 24 November 1971, received a ransom of $200,000 plus a parachute, and then baled out with the money.

Richard was also a fan of Glenn Miller and decided to follow up my researches. He came to England and located one of Britain's best known and most successful divers, Martin Woodward. We travelled down to Bembridge in the Isle of Wight, where Martin had his museum open to the public and was also building his beautiful new survey vessel *Discovery*. Over the next few

Lancaster VII serial NX611 of the Lincolnshire Aviation Heritage Centre, East Kirkby in Lincolnshire. Actors in the interior of this machine were filmed by Stone City Films for the programme *Glenn Miller's Last Flight*, shown on Channel Four Television on New Year's Eve 2001. *(Bow Watkinson collection)*

Martin Woodward in his diving gear. *(Martin Woodward collection)*

A short break in the filming of *Glenn Miller's Last Flight* by Stone City Films on behalf of Channel Four Television, at the Royal Air Force Museum on 19 September 2001. Left to right: Colin Fox (cameraman); Stratton Ritchie (interviewer); Angelique Morrison (production assistant): Bryn Higgins (producer). *(Author's collection)*

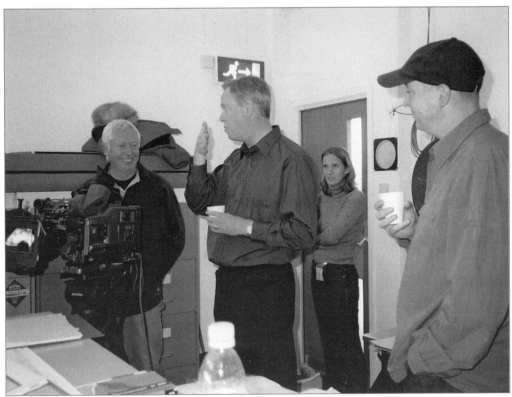

months, Martin examined my research material on Glenn Miller, checked the calculations and decided they were correct. Nevertheless, he assessed the chances of finding the remains of the Norseman in that area of the English Channel as no better than one in a thousand. After carrying out a short survey in 1993, the project was shelved.

Meanwhile, Richard and I arranged an amateur video interview with Fred Shaw at his home in Johannesburg in South Africa. This took place on 4 February 1990, carried out by some friends who were visiting South Africa, Jane and Dudley Cowderoy. The questions were written in advance by myself. Fred Shaw was always reluctant to take part in any publicity and was not in the best of health, but he replied to the questions precisely and convincingly. He died in October 1992.

There the matter rested until early 2000, when my analysis came to the attention of Channel Four Television. A meeting took place on 8 March at the Public Record Office in Kew with their Science Executive, Sarah Marris. This was followed a week later with another discussion at Channel Four's headquarters at Horseferry Road in London. After the company had examined all my evidence, Sarah and I visited Martin Woodward in the Isle of Wight on 28 July.

However, it was not until the following year that Stone City Films was appointed by Channel Four to make the programme. Some of the witnesses I had contacted were interviewed, and excerpts from the amateur video of Fred Shaw were included. Filming of dance scenes took place in Blackpool, the Lancaster at the Lincolnshire Aviation Heritage Centre was used to recreate the circumstances over the Southern Jettison Area, and other interviews were carried out underneath the Lancaster in the RAF Museum at Hendon.

Martin Woodward went out in his catamaran *Discovery* to survey the north-east quadrant of the Southern Jettison Area, for a total of four days. However, as he forecast, the venture was unsuccessful. The area proved erratic and difficult to survey, so that probably a flotilla of vessels would be required to complete the work. Even then, it seems that time and the elements have obliterated the wreckage of the fragile Norseman, and that the final evidence may never be found. The programme, entitled *Glenn Miller's Last Flight*, was shown on New Year's Eve 2001.

Sources

AMELIA EARHART

Books and articles

Air Ministry. *A.P. 1234 Air Navigation, Vol I*. London: HMSO, 1941. *A.P. 1456 Manual of Air Navigation, Vol II*. London, 1938.

Backus, John L. *Letters from Amelia*. Boston: Beacon Press, 1982.

Burke, John. *Winged Legend: The Story of Amelia Earhart*. London: Arthur Barker, 1970.

Chadwick, Roxane. *Amelia Earhart: Aviation Pioneer*. Minneapolis: Lerner, 1987.

Chichester, Francis. *Astro-navigation*. London: George Allen & Unwin, 1940.

Dwiggins, Don. *Hollywood Pilot*. New York: Doubleday, 1966.

Earhart, Amelia. *Last Flight. New York*: Harcourt Brace, 1937.

Goerner, Fred. *The Search for Amelia Earhart*. London: Bodley Head, 1966.

Long, Elgen M. and Lond, Marie K. *Amelia Earhart: The Mystery Solved*. New York: Simon & Schuster, 1999.

Loomis, Vincent and Ethell, Jeffrey. *Amelia Earhart: The Final Story*. New York: Random House, 1985.

Lovell, Mary S. *The Sound of Wings*. London: Hutchinson, 1989.

Markham, Beryl, *West with the Night*. London: Virago, 1984.

Meissner, Hans-Otto. *Inseln in der Südsee*. Munich: C. Bertelsmann, 1979.

Moolman, Valerie. *Women Aloft*. Alexandria, VA: Time-Life, 1981.

Nesbit, Roy. 'What did happen to Amelia Earhart?' *Aeroplane Monthly*, January and February 1989.

Sinclair, James. *Wings of Gold*. New York: Pacific Publications, 1978.

Strippel, Dick. *Amelia Earhart: The Myth and the Reality*. Jericho, NY, 1972.

Weems, P.V.H. *Air Navigation*. New York: McGraw-Hill, 1931.

Public Offices

British Museum Newspaper Library, Colindale

Australia	Benchmark
The Australian, Melbourne	MC758
The Courier Mail, Brisbane	MC668
Daily Telegraph, Sydney	MC565
The Melbourne Argus	MC754
The Melbourne Leader	MC770
New Zealand	
The Auckland Star	MC1000
The Evening Post, Wellington	MC960
The Press, Christchurch	MC1004
Papua New Guinea	
Papua Courier	MC931
Rabaul Times	MC934
United Kingdom	
The Daily Telegraph, London	
Daily Mail, London	
The Times, London	
USA	
San Francisco Chronicle	MA191

Public Record Office, Kew

AVIA 2/1082   Miss Amelia Earhart: proposed flight round the world, 1936–1937.
CO323/1366/1   Flight of Amelia Earhart round the world, 1936–1937.
FO 371/21541   Amelia Earhart: search for, 1938.
FO 115/3414   Aircraft: Earhart flight.

National Meteorological Archive, Bracknell
Weather reports from Nauru and Funafuti (Gilbert and Ellice Islands), 2 July 1937.

Royal Greenwich Observatory, Herstmonceaux
Altitudes and azimuths of sun near Howland Island, 2 July 1937.

AMY JOHNSON

Books and articles

'The Airspeed Oxford', *The Aeroplane*, 28 July 1937.

Bowyer, M.J.F. *Action Stations, No. 6*. Cambridge: Patrick Stephens, 1983.

British Vessels Lost at Sea. Cambridge: Patrick Stephens, 1980.

College, J.J. *Ships of the Royal Navy, Vol 2*. Newton Abbot: David & Charles, 1970.

Collier, B. *The Defence of the United Kingdom*. London: HMSO, 1957.

Curtis, Lettice. *The Forgotten Pilots*. Olney: Nelson & Saunders, 1971.

The Dictionary of National Biography, 1941–1950. London: OUP, 1950.

Duckworth, C.L.D. and Langmuir, G.E. *Railway and Other Steamers*. Glasgow: Shipping Histories, 1948.

Halpenny, B. *Action Stations, No. 8*. Cambridge: Patrick Stephens, 1984.

Kemp, P. *Oxford Companion to Ships and the Sea*. London: OUP, 1976.

King, Alison. 'Amy's Last Flight', *Aeroplane Monthly*, November and December 1980.

Lenton, H.T. and College, J.J. *Warships of World War II*. London: Ian Allan, 1964.

Lewis, P. *British Racing and Record-Breaking Aircraft*. London: Putnam, 1970.

Nesbit, Roy C. 'What Did Happen to Amy Johnson?' *Aeroplane Monthly*, January and February 1988.

Roof over Britain. London: HMSO, 1943.

Roskill, S.W. *The War at Sea, Vol. I*. London: Admiralty, 1948.

Smith, Constance Babington. *Amy Johnson*. Wellingborough: Patrick Stephens, 1988.

Taylor, H.A. *Airspeed Oxford since 1931*. London: Putnam, 1976.

The Times, 7 January 1941, 9 January 1941.

Public Offices

Aircraft A.M. Form 78, Oxford II. RAF No. V3540. Air Historical Branch.

Air Publication 1569A & B-P.N. Pilot's Notes for Oxford I & II. HMSO, 1943.

Amy Johnson File. AC77/36/1. Hendon: Royal Air Force Museum.

North Sea Pilot, Part III. London: Admiralty, 1948.

Public Record Office, Kew

ADM 1/12018	Death of Miss Amy Johnson, 5 January 1941.
ADM 199/42	1939–1941. AN, ANF, AS, BN, CW & WS Convoys – reports.
ADM 199/407	East Coast Areas: War Diaries.
ADM 199/1454	1939–1946. Nore Command War History.

AIR 13/22	Channel Convoy Logs. July 1940 – January 1941.
AIR 13/70	Admiralty Mk VI Balloons, October 1940 – May 1941.
AIR 16/365	Fighter Command, Order of Battle June 1940 – April 1942.
AIR 22/111	Air Ministry and War Room Summaries, November – December 1940.
AIR 22/112	Air Ministry and War Room Summaries, January 1941.
AIR 25/193	HQ No. 11 Group (Fighter) Operations Record Book, May 1926 – December 1941.
AIR 25/301	HQ No. 16 Group (GR) Operations Record Book, 1936 – December 1941.
AIR 25/575	HQ No. 30 Group (Balloon Barrage) Operations Record Book, January 1941 – November 1944.
AIR 27/1	No. 1 Squadron Operations Record Book, January – December 1941.
AIR 27/235	No. 17 Squadron Operations Record Book, January 1941 – December 1943.
AIR 27/425	No. 41 Squadron Operations Record Book, January 1941 – December 1943.
AIR 27/529	No. 56 Squadron Operations Record Book, January – December 1941.
AIR 27/590	No. 64 Squadron Operations Record Book, January 1941 – December 1943.
AIR 27/598	No. 66 Squadron Operations Record Book, January 1916 – December 1941.
AIR 27/641	No. 74 Squadron Operations Record Book, January 1941 – December 1942.
AIR 27/704	No. 85 Squadron Operations Record Book, January 1941 – December 1942.
AIR 27/744	No. 92 Squadron Operations Record Book, January 1941 – December 1942.
AIR 27/1471	No. 242 Squadron Operations Record Book, October 1939 – December 1942.
AIR 27/1498	No. 249 Squadron Operations Record Book, May 1940 – December 1943.
AIR 27/1511	No. 253 Squadron Operations Record Book, October 1939 – December 1943.
AIR 27/1663	No. 303 Squadron Operations Record Book, October 1940 – December 1941.
AIR 27/2069	No. 601 Squadron Operations Record Book, January – December 1941.

AIR 27/2110	No. 611 Squadron Operations Record Book, January 1941 – December 1943.
AIR 27/2123	No. 615 Squadron Operations Record Book, June 1937 – December 1943.
AIR 27/2219	No. 901 Squadron Operations Record Book, May 1938 – April 1945.
AIR 27/2221	No. 902 Squadron Operations Record Book, June 1939 – August 1944.
AIR 27/2300	No. 952 (Thames Barrage) Squadron, Operations Record Book, November 1939 – December 1941.
AIR 28/188	Debden Operations Record Book, January 1941 – June 1943.
AIR 28/384	Hornchurch Operations Record Book, October 1915 – December 1941.
AIR 28/601	Northolt Operations Record Book, January 1915 – December 1945.
AIR 28/603	North Weald Operations Record Book, September 1927 – December 1945.
AIR 28/724	Squires Gate Operations Record Book, December 1940 – October 1945.
AIR 29/1003	No. 45 MU Operations Record Book, April 1940 – December 1946.
AIR 29/562	Kidlington Operations Record Book, May 1939 – June 1945.
AIR 29/613	Hatfield Operations Record Book, November 1940 – April 1947.
AIR 41/1	Balloon Defences, 1914–1945.
WO 166/2348	58th (Kent) Heavy AA Regt, War Diary, September 1939 – December 1941.

Weather Reports. 27 December 1940 and 5 January 1941. Bracknell: National Meteorological Archive.

BEAUFORTS UNDER WATER

Books and articles

'Divers to Hunt for Beaufort', *Royal Air Force News*, 24 June 1992.

'A Brush with the Past', *Royal Air Force News*, 17 September 1993.

'The Seabed Yields its War Wreckage', *Malta Independent*, 29 November 1992.

'Vandals Destroy War Relic that Time Preserved', *Malta Independent*, 18 July 1993.

'Beaufort W6498', Valletta: *Sub*, June 1992.

Besley, James. 'Puzzle of the Heroic Airman', Bristol: *Evening Post*, 22 July 1991.

Botham, J.A. *Böröy Beaufort*. Unpublished. 27 September 1991.

Hayward, Roger. *The Beaufort File*. Tonbridge: Air Britain, 1990.

Larsen, Jan Harald. *Her ligg flyraket*. Norway: Bömlo-nytt, 15 November 1991.

Nesbit, Roy C. 'RAFSAA Expedition to Norway', *Air Clues*, June 1992.

Nesbit, Roy C. 'Hunt for a Beaufort', *Aeroplane Monthly*, October 1991.

Nesbit, Roy C. 'Brush with the Past', *Air Clues*, December 1993.

Royal Air Force Sub-Aqua Association. *Expedition Report: Malta 11–25 October 1992*. Unpublished.

Public Offices

Bömlo Kommune; National Meteorological Archive; Royal Air Force Sub-Aqua Association; Royal Air Force Museum, Accident Card Beaufort IA serial DW805.

Public Record Office

AIR 22/118	Air Ministry and War Room Summaries, July 1941.
AIR 22/119	Air Ministry and War Room Summaries, August 1941.
AIR 25/380	No. 18 Group Operations Record Book, September 1939 – December 1943.
AIR 27/435	No. 42 Squadron Operations Record Book, April 1916 – December 1941.
AIR 27/436	No. 42 Squadron Operations Record Book, January 1942 – December 1943.
AIR 28/503	Luqa Operations Record Book, January – December 1942.
AIR 29/471	Overseas Aircraft Despatch Unit, December 1941 – April 1945.

THE DUKE OF KENT

Books

Barker, Ralph. *Great Mysteries of the Air*. London: Chatto & Windus, 1966.

Evans, John. *The Sunderland: Flying Boat Queen*. Pembroke Dock: Paterchurch Publications, 1987.

Jones, A.C. Merton. *British Independent Airlines since 1946*. Vol. 4. Liverpool: Mersey Aviation Society, 1977.

Roskill, S.W. *The War at Sea*, Vol. I, London: HMSO, 1954.

The Dictionary of National Biography, 1941–1950. London: OUP, 1959.

Hansard, Volume 384, Session 1941–42.

Who Was Who, Volume IV. London: Adam & Charles Black, 1952.

Who Was Who, Volume V. London: Adam & Charles Black, 1961.

Articles

The Times, 26–28 August, 1942.

Crowther, Chris. 'Disaster Royal', *Aeroplane Monthly*, January 1983.

McWhirter, Robin. 'The Tragedy at Eagle's Rock', *The Scotsman*, August 1985.

Smith, David J. 'The Death of the Duke of Kent', *After the Battle*, Issue No. 37, 1982.

Nesbit, Roy. 'What Did Happen to the Duke of Kent? Part One', *Aeroplane Monthly*, January 1990.

Nesbit, Roy. 'What Did Happen to the Duke of Kent? Part Two', *Aeroplane Monthly*, February 1990.

Mr Pepys's Page. 'Riddle of the Dead Duke', *London Evening Standard*, 16 January 1990.

Londoner's Diary. 'Cousin Told how Prince Georgie Died', *London Evening Standard*, 26 January 1990.

Correspondence, *Aeroplane Monthly*, April 1990.

Nesbit, Roy C. 'Duke of Kent Update', *Aeroplane Monthly*, March 1992.

Nesbit, Roy C. 'A Travesty of the Truth', *Aeroplane Monthly*, September 1996.

Public Offices

Admiralty Compass Observatory, Ditton Park. Correspondence.

Air Historical Branch, MoD, Aircraft Accident Card, Sunderland III W4026.

British Geological Survey, Edinburgh. Correspondence.

Meteorological Archives, Bracknell. Weather reports, 24–25 August, 1942.

Public Record Office, Kew

ADM 1/11937	Death of the Duke of Kent, 1942.
AIR 2/6470	Court mourning and flags at half-mast.
AIR 2/16973	Dr J.R. Kennedy, Gallantry Award.
AIR 10/2444	AP1566C Sunderland III, May 1942.
AIR 10/2445	AP1566C Sunderland III, November 1942.
AIR 25/418	18 Group Operations Record Book, Appendices, August 1942.
AIR 27/1413	228 Squadron Operations Record Book, January –December 1940.
AIR 27/1414	228 Squadron Operations Record Book, January – December 1941.

AIR 27/1415	228 Squadron Operations Record Book, January –December 1942.
AIR 28/402	Invergordon Narrative. September 1939 – December 1942.
AIR 28/620	Oban Operations Record Book, September 1939 – December 1942.
AIR 28/915	Wick Operations Record Book, September 1939 – December 1943.
AIR 29/1013	56 MU Operations Record Book, November 1940 – November 1945.
HO 45/20275	Death of HRH The Duke of Kent.
PREM 4/8/2A	The Duke of Kent.

Radio Scotland, *The Crash of W-4206*, broadcast 26 August 1985.

Royal Air Force Museum, Hendon
AP1234 Air Navigation, 1943.
AP2544A, Volume I, ASV Mk II, Equipment & Ancillaries, 1943.
Radio & Navigation Systems, BOAC, c. 1950.

GLENN MILLER

Books and articles

The Aeroplane, 'The Viking Spirit', 6 January 1936.
The Aeroplane, 'Air Transport Ice', 29 December 1944.
Barker, R. *Great Mysteries of the Air*. London: Chatto & Windus, 1966.
Bowyer, M.F.J. *Action Stations No. 1*. Cambridge: Patrick Stephens, 1979.
Bowyer, M.F.J. *Action Stations No. 6*. Cambridge: Patrick Stephens, 1983.
Butcher, G. *Next to a Letter from Home*. Edinburgh: Mainstream, 1986.
Flight, 'Ice Formation in Carburettors', 14 February 1945.
Flight, 'Ice Formation', 25 February 1941.
Flight, 'The Icing Problem', 20 November 1941.
Flight, 'Carburettor Ice Scoops', 17 September 1942.
Longmate, N. *The Doodlebugs*. London: Hutchinson, 1981.
MacDonald, C.B. *The Battle of the Bulge*. London: Weidenfeld & Nicolson, 1984.
Middlebrook, M. and Everitt, G. *The Bomber Command War Diaries*. Harmondsworth: Viking, 1985.
Nesbit, Roy. 'What Did Happen to Glenn Miller?' *Aeroplane Monthly*, January and February 1987.
Simon, G.T. *Glenn Miller and his Orchestra*. London: W.H. Allen, 1974.
Titler, D.M. *Wings of Mystery*. New York: Dodd, Mead & Co., 1981.

Public Offices

Air Publication 1661B. Armament, November 1947.

Notes issued to US Bomb Disposal Personnel, 1945.

National Meteorological Archive: Weather Report, 15 December 1944.

Public Record Office, Kew

ADM 1/15954	Complaints made to US authorities concerning jettisoning of bombs by US aircraft near British ships and defences. Steps taken to prevent this, 1944.
AIR 10/3712	AP3040. Notes on the compilation of the Operations Record Book, December 1943.
AIR 10/4038	Airfields.
AIR 14/233	Routeing of aircraft: tactical planning, June 1942 – April 1945.
AIR 14/1353	Target routeing and signals, October 1943 – October 1944.
AIR 14/3129	Group Operational Orders, December 1944.
AIR 14/3457	Reports on Operational Sorties, September 1944 – December 1944.
AIR 20/7586	Airfields.
AIR 22/139	Air Ministry and War Room Summaries, December 1944 – January 1945.
AIR 22/158	Air Ministry, States of Operational Squadrons, September 1944 – December 1944.
AIR 24/301	Bomber Command Operations Record Book, Appendices, December 1944.
AIR 24/302	Bomber Command Operations Record Book, Appendices, December 1944.
AIR 24/303	Bomber Command Operations Record Book, Appendices, December 1944.
AIR 24/1496	2nd TAF Operations Record Book, June 1943 – December 1944.
AIR 25/53	No. 3 Group Operations Record Book, January 1944 – December 1944.
AIR 25/80	No. 3 Group Operations Record Book, Appendices, November – December 1944.
AIR 25/195	No. 11 Group Operations Record Book, January 1944 – December 1944.
AIR 25/217	No. 11 Group Operations Record Book, Appendices, December 1944.

AIR 25/303	No. 16 Group Operations Record Book, January 1944 – December 1944.
AIR 25/381	No. 18 Group Operations Record Book, January 1944 – December 1944.
AIR 25/777	No. 100 Group Operations Record Book, December 1943 – December 1945.
AIR 25/783	No. 100 Group Operations Record Book, December 1944 – January 1945.

Lancaster Squadrons

AIR 27/204	No. 15 Squadron Operations Record Book, January 1944 – December 1944.
AIR 27/207	No. 15 Squadron Operations Record Book, Appendices, May 1940 – June 1945.
AIR 27/647	No. 75 Squadron Operations Record Book, January 1944 – December 1944.
AIR 27/649	No. 75 Squadron Operations Record Book, Appendices, April 1940 – January 1945.
AIR 27/732	No. 90 Squadron Operations Record Book, January 1944 – December 1944.
AIR 27/737	No. 90 Squadron Operations Record Book, Appendices, August 1940 – April 1945.
AIR 27/892	No. 115 Squadron Operations Record Book, August 1944 – December 1944.
AIR 27/1004	No. 149 Squadron Operations Record Book, August 1944 – May 1945.
AIR 27/1006	No. 149 Squadron Operations Record Book, Appendices, January 1941 – April 1945.
AIR 27/1145	No. 186 Squadron Operations Record Book, April 1943 – June 1945.
AIR 27/1146	No. 186 Squadron Operations Record Book, Appendices, December 1944 – April 1945.
AIR 27/1164	No. 195 Squadron Operations Record Book, November 1942 – August 1945.
AIR 27/1165	No. 195 Squadron Operations Record Book, Appendices, December 1944 – April 1945.
AIR 27/1352	No. 218 Squadron Operations Record Book, January– December 1944.
AIR 27/1358	No. 514 Squadron Operations Record Book, Appendices, December 1944.

AIR 27/1978   No. 514 Squadron Operations Record Book, July 1944 – December 1944.

AIR 27/1980   No. 514 Squadron Operations Record Book, Appendices, November 1943 – April 1945.

AIR 27/2138   No. 622 Squadron Operations Record Book, July – December 1944.

Mustang Squadrons

AIR 27/254   No. 19 Squadron Operations Record Book, January 1944 – December 1945.

AIR 27/591   No. 64 Squadron Operations Record Book, January 1944 – December 1945.

AIR 27/595   No. 65 Squadron Operations Record Book, January 1944 – December 1945.

AIR 27/915   No. 122 Squadron Operations Record Book, May 1941 – February 1946.

AIR 27/927   No. 126 Squadron Operations Record Book, January 1944 – March 1946.

AIR 27/934   No. 129 Squadron Operations Record Book, June 1941 – March 1946.

AIR 27/1440   No. 234 Squadron Operations Record Book, January 1944 – August 1946.

AIR 27/1674   No. 306 Squadron Operations Record Book, January 1944 – December 1946.

AIR 27/1679   No. 309 Squadron Operations Record Book, October 1940 – December 1946.

AIR 27/1701   No. 315 Squadron Operations Record Book, January 1944 – December 1946.

AIR 27/1705   No. 316 Squadron Operations Record Book, January 1944 – November 1946.

Air-Sea Rescue Squadrons

AIR 27/1610   No. 279 Squadron Operations Record Book, January 1944 – September 1945.

AIR 27/1612   No. 280 Squadron Operations Record Book, January 1944 – May 1945.

AIR 27/1615   No. 282 Squadron Operations Record Book, January 1943 – July 1945.

Stations

AIR 28/146	Chedburgh Operations Record Book, June 1945 – November 1946.
AIR 28/148	Chedburgh Operations Record Book, Appendices, October 1944 – October 1946.
AIR 28/532	Mepal Operations Record Book, June 1943 – June 1945.
AIR 28/538	Methwold Operations Record Book, January 1944 – April 1946.
AIR 28/539	Methwold Operations Record Book, Appendices, November 1943 – October 1945.
AIR 28/547	Mildenhall Operations Record Book, January 1943 – December 1945.
AIR 28/859	Tuddenham Operations Record Book, October 1943 – December 1945.
AIR 28/860	Tuddenham Operations Record Book, Appendices, October 1943 – December 1945.
AIR 28/889	Waterbeach Operations Record Book, March 1941 – December 1945.
AIR 28/893	Waterbeach Operations Record Book, Appendices, May 1944 – August 1945.
AIR 28/949	Witchford Operations Record Book, January 1943 – March 1946.
AIR 28/959	Wratting Common Operations Record Book, November 1944 – April 1946.
AIR 28/960	Wratting Common Operations Record Book, June 1943 – March 1946.
AIR 29/680	Twinwood Farm Operations Record Book, July 1941 – June 1945.

Air-Sea Rescue Marine Craft Units

AIR 29/443	No. 24 ASRMU Operations Record Book, October 1943 – May 1945.
AIR 29/444	No. 26 ASRMU Operations Record Book, September 1943 – August 1945.
AIR 29/445	No. 27 ASRMU Operations Record Book, December 1940 – November 1945.
AIR 29/446	No. 28 ASRMU Operations Record Book, July 1940 – July 1946.
	No. 30 ASRMU Operations Record Book, September 1939 – February 1945.
	No. 32 ASRMU Operations Record Book, April 1944 – October 1945.
AIR 29/447	No. 40 ASRMU Operations Record Book, April 1944 – June 1946.

US Eighth Air Force

AIR 40/780   Operations, December 1944.

AIR 40/1092   Daily Narrative of Operations, May 1944 – May 1945.

Flying Bombs

WO 199/553   'Diver', June 1944 – October 1944.

Index